SHIPS

A CONCISE GUIDE IN COLOUR

SHIPS

by Ing. Jaromír Kozák

*Illustrated by Přemysl Pospíšil
and Miroslav Rada*

Hamlyn
London · New York · Sydney · Toronto

Translated by Jan Hrůša and Daniela Coxon
Designed and produced by Artia for
THE HAMLYN PUBLISHING GROUP LIMITED
London · New York · Sydney · Toronto
Hamlyn House, Feltham, Middlesex, England
Copyright © Artia 1973

ISBN 0 600 37972 8
Printed in Czechoslovakia

CONTENTS

EVEN SHIPS HAVE A HISTORY

Ships or water craft, in the broader sense of the word, are the oldest means of transport. Their gradual development can be traced back with available historical evidence, 6,000 years. Drawings on archeological finds testify to the existence of ships as early as 8,000 to 10,000 years ago. Although it is not known exactly whether it was a tree trunk, a raft, a bundle of reeds, or an inflated animal skin that first provided man with water transport, the shape of the oldest vessels can be reconstructed from ships built subsequently and from those still used by primitive peoples. These ships have in many cases not changed for centuries and meet the needs of contemporary primitive tribes just as well as they did those of their ancestors.

The actual point in time when man first started to use the power of the wind and invented the sail, cannot be fixed. Whether he was inspired by a bundle of branches or a floating twig, stirred by the wind, or whether he conceived the idea after he had accidentally stretched out a skin or mat, is unknown. Ships proved their worth mainly in forested and desert regions, where flowing water was the only means of transport. A tree trunk hollowed out by a crude chisel or fire, became a boat, used simply as it was or provided with an outrigger to improve its stability. Such craft were operated by paddles, oars or by sail and are still used for river and sea navigation in South America and Asia and among the islands of the Pacific Ocean. The use of such boats in prehistoric times has been confirmed by the remains of partially hollowed-out trunks, called dug-outs, found in the sand and mud deposits of large river basins on all continents. Subsequently, by joining a number of logs together a raft was constructed, and rafts, as a means of transporting timber, still survive in countries with large expanses of water and timber industries, although such rafts have naturally been modernised. Tree trunks are joined into long sections and towed through the water by tugs to the next processing point. Rafts have also been used for sailing on the high seas and the theory that some of the islands in the Pacific Ocean were settled by the inhabitants of South America has been proved in part by the exploits of the Norwegian ethnographer, Thor Heyerdahl, who undertook such a voyage on a balsa raft.

Another type of raft is that made of inflated animal skins, joined together over a wooden skeleton. They are commonplace among South American and Asiatic peoples and are found on the large rivers of China and Mesopotamia. Also to be found among those primitive vessels that have been preserved from prehistoric times to the present day, are circular boats woven from reeds and sealed by bitumen or sheathed in animal skins. They come from the river basins of the Euphrates and the Tigris. There are also boats constructed from reeds, whose original home was Egypt and which are still in use in Ethiopia and on Lake Titicaca in South America. Oval-shaped coracles, covered by skins, are also woven from reeds. They were used by the Ancient Britons and are still used by fishermen in Ireland and Wales. Similarly, the canoes and kayaks of the old inhabitants of North America and Greenland must be counted as primitive vessels. They have a wooden or bone skeleton and are sheathed by tree bark or skins. A further craft in this category is the junk, which has not changed its shape for centuries and, because of its navigability, is still one of the best vessels of Eastern Asia.

The development of shipbuilding and of sea and river navigation was concentrated in the very places which proved the cultural birthplace of mankind. The oldest traces have been found in the Middle East, where excavated material dating from *circa* 5000 BC has facilitated the study of the techniques of wooden shipbuilding on the Euphrates, Tigris and Nile rivers. Such ships had a flat bottom and were propelled by oars or paddles. In the third millennium BC, sea-going, keeled ships began to appear in the Mediterranean, and the use of sails for their propulsion dates from approximately the same period.

ANCIENT VESSELS

Egypt

Reports and drawings found on papyrus and monuments as well as finds made in the pyramids, indicate that the oldest Egyptian vessels were made from bundles of a certain type of reed, papyrus. Later, wooden ships were built from local materials, such as acacia bushes and sycamore trees, which provided only short timbers. These vessels were wide, flat-bottomed and employed sails, dependent on the north-westerly winds, for sailing down the Nile, and oars were used for progress upstream. Such structural parts of a ship as the keel, posts and ribs were unknown to Egyptian shipbuilders of this period. It was only in the middle of the third millennium BC, when cedar wood was imported from Lebanon, that bigger and more sophisticated ships began to appear, built with a long, rising bow and stern, which made them suitable for sea navigation. One to three wide oars were loosely suspended on both sides of the ship and were used for steering. The bodywork was strengthened by a hawser, which encircled the upper part of the hull. The decoration of such ships was very lavish. Both bow and stern terminated in the shape of the very popular lotus flower. These ships were first propelled by paddles, later by oars assisted by a single square sail, which was made of papyrus or linen. In vessels of the earlier period the sail was fixed to a double tabernacle mast, which could be tilted towards the stern, whereas in those of a later date the mast was fixed and the sail could be hauled down.

The zenith of Egyptian sea transport was reached around 1500 BC in the reign of Queen Hatshepsut and the Pharaoh Thutmose III and was closely connected to the development of Egyptian commerce in the Mediterranean. Design changes that followed affected masts and sails, while free steering oars were replaced by oars with tillers, fixed to both sides of the stern. Ships were also being adapted for war. Oarsmen were shielded by side planking, platforms with superstructures or shelters were

9

built fore and aft, and crow's nests were placed at the top of the masts. This type of Egyptian ship is depicted on a frieze in the temple of Amon in Medinet Hab near Thebes, which illustrates a battle against northern invaders in the Nile delta, in the reign of Ramses III in 1197 BC.

The Nile was the main navigation route of the Ancient Egyptians and even 5,000 years ago stone from Aswan was being transported down river. The Red Sea and the eastern Mediterranean were also within their orbit. Trading expeditions in the Mediterranean, mainly to Crete and Phoenicia were quite common. In the twelfth century BC further changes in ship design took place and the square sail of Egyptian ships lost its lower yard, thus rounding off its development.

In the course of the first millennium BC other Mediterranean nations tackled the art of shipbuilding, the most famous of which were the Phoenicians and later the Greeks, whose services were even employed by the Egyptian Pharaohs.

At the beginning of the sixth century BC, for example, the Pharaoh Necho sent a fleet, built by Greek architects and manned by a Phoenician crew, on a long voyage. According to the historian Herodotus, these ships succeeded in sailing round Africa for the first time. A further spur to the development of Egyptian shipping was the construction of a canal connecting the Mediterranean to the Red Sea. The building of this canal began during the reign of Ptolemy II in 285 BC and it remained navigable until the fourteenth century.

Phoenicia and Assyria

Thanks to the favourable position of their country, the Phoenicians became famous as excellent sailors throughout the Mediterranean where they sailed not to rob or conquer but to trade. They most probably absorbed the navigational experience of the Egyptians and the Cretans, although little is known about the latter's ships apart from a few pictures on seals. According to Herodotus the Phoenicians were the first to dare to sail on the open sea. Hitherto ships had sailed, even for long distances, within sight of the coast and only during daylight. A knowledge of astronomy and the quality of Phoenician ships, which had keels, frames and two banks of oars, made it possible for them to penetrate far to the west, through the Straits of Gibraltar and to establish trading colonies in the places they reached. The best known of such colonies were on the islands of Cyprus, Rhodes, Malta and Sicily, whilst the largest colony on the African coast was Carthage and on the Spanish coast, Cadiz. In the fifth century BC a Carthaginian sailor, called Hannon, set out on an expedition with sixty large ships, driven by oars, and founded colonies on the west coast of Africa. So in the first millennium BC the Phoenicians were generally famous as sailors and their fleet was much greater than Egypt's, both in terms of quality and in numbers of ships. The voyages of the Carthaginians extended northwards from Gibraltar to the southern coasts of England and to the North Sea from where tin and amber were increasingly imported.

Further information on primitive sailing techniques has been found in the area around present-day Iraq, which was formerly Babylonia and Assyria; countries which controlled even Phoenicia at one time. In the ruins of the palace of the Assyrian King Sargon II in Chorsabad, built about 700 BC, reliefs have been found showing cargo ships, probably Phoenician, transporting timber both on their decks and by towing. Similarly voyages on inflated animal skins and rafts, made of the same material, were illustrated. In ancient Nineveh, in the ruins of the Nimrud palace, friezes have been discovered showing sailing on the Euphrates and Tigris rivers. The craft were warships whose keel extended into the powerful protruding ram. They were propelled by oars and eventually by a single rectangular sail. The ships were steered by means of two oar-type rudders, suspended from the sides aftwards. The rowers were protected by a wooden side planking and the warriors, on the upper deck, sheltered behind round bucklers.

Greece

The navigation and shipbuilding experience of the Phoenicians
and the inhabitants of the Aegean islands was absorbed by the
Greeks for whom the indented coastline of the Peloponnese,
Asia Minor and the numerous offshore islands of the Aegean,
provided many excellent harbours and anchorages. From the
eighth century onwards the Greeks started to move from such
overcrowded areas and found colonies all over the Mediterranean. Their ships, the appearance of which we know from
their pottery, mosaics, reliefs and written evidence, were originally, in the eleventh century BC, uncovered, without decks and
had flat bottoms so that they could be easily pulled on shore.
Both stern and bow were rounded off; the sternpost terminated
in a spiral crest, whilst the stempost took the form of a bird's
head.

Ships of a later period were given decks, and the oaken keel
ended in a long bow ram. The rest of the ship was made out
of fir and the planks and ribs were held together by flat wooden
nails. Unseasoned timber was often used in shipbuilding and
consequently the life of such ships was short. Greek ships were
famous as warships, particularly after the defeat of the Persians
at Salamis in 480 BC, and also as transport vessels. In the latter
capacity Alexander the Great used them to sail to India in the
heyday of Greek sea power.

A credible enough picture of the appearance of Greek vessels
can be reconstructed from surviving documents. They had
a wooden frame and their warships had oars, commonly arranged in banks one above the other. The ratio of length to
beam was 7:1 in warships, and 3:1 in cargo vessels. Transports
used sails for propulsion, as a rule one square sail attached to
a mast firmly fixed amidships and later a smaller square sail
on an inclined mast in the bow. Usually, even warships had one
square sail, which was used, however, only on long voyages.
When hugging the coast and during battle manoeuvres, this
mast was taken down and, because of the shortage of space, was

left ashore. The average length of Greek ships was 115 feet (35 metres), the beam was 40 feet (12 metres) and the depth was 16½ feet (5 metres), which meant that their displacement ranged from 700 to 800 tons. Such ships already had iron anchors, though still with wooden shafts, and a rudder, although this still took the form of wide oars, suspended from the side of the vessel and attached to a tiller to achieve better control. To make navigation safer lighthouses were built on prominent places along the coast.

In Greek ships the art of ancient shipbuilding in the Mediterranean reached its zenith. Further development was hindered by the sail and steering techniques and also the size of harbour of the period. In one instance, however, the Greeks illustrated their shipbuilding potential. According to Plutarch, Hieron, King of Syracuse, ordered a ship to be built as a gift for the Egyptian Pharaoh, Ptolemy II. The ship was described as having twenty banks of oars. Her architect was Archimedes. Her displacement was claimed to be 6,000 tons. She had three decks, a sports area, a swimming pool, gardens, a picture gallery, workshops, and stalls, and was richly decorated. She was named *Syracusia* and set sail for Alexandria, which was the only town that had a suitable harbour for such a great ship. The records do not say anything more about the fate of this ship.

Rome

For a long time the Romans were mainly engaged in agriculture and had little interest in navigation. Their poorly indented coastline did not provide good harbours; even the famous harbour of Ostia was very often blocked by the sands of the Tiber and was in any case mainly used by foreigners. The struggle for the sea only started in the third century BC during the conflict with Carthage over Sicily. From the seventh century BC Carthage had been a centre of culture and trade in the Mediterranean. The Romans, however, eventually built up a powerful navy, the basis of which were ships designed on the lines of an accidentally-captured Carthaginian vessel. They modified such ships from their experience of land warfare, equipping them with drawbridges for hooking enemy vessels. The ship's towers were equipped with catapults similar to those used on land. By using such techniques the Romans succeeded in defeating the Carthaginians in the Battle of Mylae in 260 BC. However Rome did not dominate the whole of the Mediterranean until after the annihilation of Carthage in 146 BC during the Third Punic War.

After the defeat of Carthage, Rome had no more need for warships and the trireme, built according to the Greek and Carthaginian models, once again became the main type of vessel in the Mediterranean. She was, however, far bigger and clumsier than before. The increase in maritime trade and the decline of Roman sea power encouraged piracy to such an extent that by the first century BC trade routes to Rome were being menaced. The Romans succeeded in liquidating most of this piracy by 67 BC because they had developed a new type of fast warship, the liburn. These ships were built along the lines of those used by the pirates of the Dalmatian coast. They were slender, light and generally single-bank rowing vessels, with a square sail and were easy to steer. In addition to a bow ram, liburns were equipped with catapults. They proved themselves once more in the Battle of Actium in 31 BC when they formed the backbone of Octavian's fleet, while that of Antony and Cleopatra was mainly composed of heavy multi-banked ships.

The further the Roman Empire expanded, the greater became the significance of navigation. Rome imported a number of products from neighbouring countries and islands, including cereals, cattle, fruit, oil, wine, cloth, jewels, and building materials. Small merchant ships were used for carrying such goods over short distances. Their length was about 22 yards and their beam 3.3 yards. This international trade became the foundation of Rome's wealth and extended over the whole of the known world, from China to the North Sea, from Gaul to the Black Sea and the Danube valley. Harbours were excavated and enlarged, and regular communications were established with the Roman provinces. Shipowners became the most honoured and privileged section of the population. Even if the Romans did not contribute significantly to the architecture of ships, they gained fame as good sailors, navigation experts and colonisers. They contributed not only to the advances in seafaring but were also responsible for the introduction of river navigation on the Rhine, Rhône and Danube.

Byzantium

After the collapse of the Roman Empire in c. AD 476 the western Mediterranean gradually became dominated by North African and Iberian Arabic peoples, while in the eastern Mediterranean the sea power of the Eastern Roman or Byzantine Empire developed and expanded. The centre of trade and culture was Constantinople, founded by Greek settlers in 657 BC. The design of merchant ships remained in principle unchanged for a long time but permanent conflict with the Saracen invaders, who dominated the southern coast of the Mediterranean, led to changes in warships. Naval triremes and the light, speedy liburns were replaced by a new vessel called the dromon. The dromons were slender, fast ships with two banks of oars, twenty-five in each, which were located in the ship's hull. Fore and aft they were rigged with two, later three to four masts, set with lateen sails. The masts were of the tabernacle type although they remained fixed. The sides of the ship were metal-plated, the keel extended into a bow ram and their main weapon was 'Greek Fire', a mixture of sulphur, oil, saltpetre and resin, which was catapulted from a bellows-operated projector in the bow on to the enemy vessels. Such war inventions helped the Byzantine Empire maintain its sea power until the twelfth century when the sea became dominated by the Italian towns of Genoa and Venice.

Dromons were subdivided into various classes which differed from each other in the number of oarsmen per bank of oars.

The number of oars remained the same as did the approximate length of such ships, namely 130 feet (42 metres). Dromons inherited the speed of the liburns and their fighting power was also in keeping with that of ancient warships. As well as dromons there were smaller warships, called pamfils, and galleys which had a single bank of oars, one lateen sail and an afterdeck.

MEDIEVAL SHIPS

Viking Ships

Rock paintings from the Bronze Age, discovered in East Gotland in southern Sweden, indicate that the inhabitants of the Baltic coast tackled the problems of navigation and shipbuilding some time before Christ and in a much stormier sea than the Mediterranean. In comparison with Mediterranean vessels those of the Scandinavians were equipped with sails and consequently their sailors must have known how to tack against the wind. During their conquest in the last century before Christ, the Romans, using their heavy, cumbersome war galleys, confronted the Scandinavians, who resisted Roman naval power for a long time as the oaken hull of the northern ships stood up well to the battering ram. Only when the Romans cut the ropes holding the Scandinavians' sails, thus making it impossible for them to manoeuvre, did they defeat them. The main development in navigation in the north took place between the fifth and eleventh centuries AD, when the Vikings, the Germanic ancestors of contemporary Danes and Norwegians, dominated the maritime areas of northern Europe, penetrated the Baltic Sea and, using the rivers, sailed deep into the heart of Russia. They conquered and colonised parts of England, discovered and settled in Iceland and Greenland and, about the year AD 1000, reached North America and named the territory of present-day New Foundland, Vinland. Their ships differed substantially from the vessels used in the Mediterranean. They were slender, had ribs, were clinker-built (with overlapping planks) and double-ended. They were propelled either by one square sail, made of skin, or by one bank of oars. They were called 'long ships'. Oared ships were used mainly for coastal voyages. Viking warships reached 140 feet (46 metres) in length and had up to 34 rowers on either side. Their cargo ships were rounder, about 66 feet long by 16.5 feet wide and in contrast to the warships had a fixed mast.

The Mediterranean

The crusades had a considerable impact on the development of shipbuilding from the eleventh to the thirteenth centuries. At that time throughout western Europe and particularly in the Mediterranean the importance of towns was gradually increasing as a direct consequence of the expansion of trade and urban craftsmanship. By the thirteenth century Venice had become the richest town in Europe and dominated the maritime trade of the Mediterranean. A typical vessel of this period, designed for war, was the rowing galley, which was a lineal descendent of Greek triremes, Dalmatian liburns and Byzantine dromons. It was rigged with lateen sails and fitted with a robust steering mechanism. Sailing vessels similar to Roman types were still used for local trade voyages. The only development was that square sails were replaced by lateen sails as a result of Byzantine influence. These ships had to be adapted for the crusades, which involved the transportation of a great number of people, horses and stores. At first the bow and stern did not differ very much from each other; the shape of the vessels only became more circular and their size increased. According to surviving charts from the middle of the thirteenth century, the waterline length was almost 105 feet and their moulded beam was some 43 feet. Fore and aft, huge, levelled superstructures called castles, similar to the towers of older warships, developed from a simple railed platform. These castles also overhung the main contours of the hull. The depth from the keel to the highest deck of the castle was often 40 feet, whilst the draught was roughly 19 feet. The forecastle narrowed towards the prow and later gave rise to the beak-head, a typical feature of the multi-deck sailing vessel of the sixteenth and seventeenth centuries. The castles provided the accommodation for the crew, the ship's master, the passengers and soldiers. Animals and stores were placed below deck. A loading bay with a boarding platform was cut into the side of the ship for taking on horses. The sides of the vessel were fitted with bulwarks, which had portholes and from which were suspended the coats of arms of the nobility. The larger vessels had cabins for passengers along the sides of the upper deck so that their roofs formed a continuous inner gallery around the whole ship.

These ships had a solid framing, with a short bowsprit protruding from the bow. One high mast was located amidships and aloft it carried the usual crow's nest. The ship was steered by means of two steering oars protruding from the sides at the stern and controlled from the sterncastle. These vessels had no special name but were known as 'nef', 'nave' or 'nao'.

At the end of the twelfth century navigation between Christian nations had been resumed throughout the whole of the Mediterranean. The crusades also helped to renew trade links between the Mediterranean and the North Sea. In peace time a great many pilgrims sailed to the Holy Land from all over Europe and from the Near East oriental luxury goods were transported to enrich the markets of European towns. Between the thirteenth and fifteenth centuries sailing techniques developed further and ships were improved. The lateen sail on the high mast was replaced by a big square one, and during the thirteenth century most ships acquired a second, generally taller mast, which was situated nearer the prow. This, and the new centrally aligned stern rudder, considerably improved the manoeuvrability of craft. The idea of the stern rudder spread from the Atlantic and reached the Mediterranean by the middle of the thirteenth century where it quickly became popular. At the end of the fifteenth century a third mast, inclined forwards and provided with a small square sail, occasionally appeared on the bow.

This period also witnessed advances in the art of navigation. Hitherto only experienced sailors could cross great stretches of water, using the heavenly bodies to guide them; during the day they generally used the sun and at night familiar stars. In the twelfth century knowledge of the compass reached the Mediterranean. The idea originated in China in the third century AD and was used by Arabic navigators in the ninth century AD. In the fifteenth century the Portuguese adapted the astrolabe for navigation at sea. Coastal sailing developed into real sea navigation. The first voyages of discovery were along the African coast and were directed by Henry the Navigator. Before long, sea travel and such voyages became the preserve of nations settled along the Atlantic seaboard.

The North and Baltic Seas

Developments in shipping in the Mediterranean provoked a response in north-western Europe. In the eleventh and twelfth centuries progress was mainly concentrated in the area of the North Sea. This coincided with the increasing importance of the harbour towns of Friesland and Flanders and along the Rhine in Saxony. The town of Bruges became an entrepôt for England, while on the Rhine the main trading centre was Cologne, which could be reached by sea-going vessels of the period. A common type of ship in use was one similar to the Viking long ship, which the Normans adapted as a transport vessel, slightly increasing its size in the process. Later the task of merchant shipping was taken over by a rounder type of vessel, employed in the coastal trade around the Frisian islands. In comparison with the Mediterranean ships, these vessels had a stronger frame and were more seaworthy. They were clinker-built, had a massive keel, a raised stempost, a continuous deck and amidships one high mast with a square sail. Similar to such Frisian ships was a type of river craft used on the lower Rhine and Meuse, called hulks, and mainly used for transporting wine and cereals.

From the middle of the thirteenth century, as indicated on town seals and the friezes of buildings, the stern rudder began to appear, controlled by a hand tiller, and also platforms, both fore and aft, which were the predecessors of later castles. The hitherto identical shape of the bow and the stern began to change; the prow became spoon-shaped, while the stern was adapted to take the stern rudder and carried a huge superstructure, the castle. This type of ship, appropriate for the needs of the Middle Ages, was named the cog, after the wine barrels that it originally carried.

At the beginning of the fourteenth century cogs arrived in the Mediterranean where they gradually replaced the large crusader ships. Initially cogs had one more mast, aft, set with a lateen sail and later a third mast, fore, which had a smaller square sail. They became the main cargo vessel of the fourteenth to sixteenth centuries, operating in the Atlantic Ocean, and the North and Baltic Seas, from where they sailed on trading expeditions all the way to Novgorod in central Russia.

Great advances in navigation and maritime trade were generated in this area by the association of coastal towns, called the Hanseatic League, which was established in 1241 and which survived until the middle of the seventeenth century. During this period all the well known harbour towns and certain inland ones near the North and Baltic Seas became involved in this venture. The most famous Hanseatic towns were Bremen, Hamburg, Bergen, Lübeck, Wismar and Stralsund. Hanseatic cogs, indigenous to this area, operated in the Atlantic and the Mediterranean. The main centres for the building of cogs were the Hanseatic towns of Wismar and Lübeck, where, incidentally, the name, cog, remained in use the longest.

NEW AGE SHIPS

The Age of Transoceanic Discoveries

The countries of the Iberian peninsula, around which the northern cogs sailed to the Mediterranean and the Mediterranean nefs to the Atlantic Ocean and the North Sea, had the most advantageous conditions for maritime exploration. In these countries the knowledge of navigation and experiments in the art of shipbuilding became interdependent. The first voyages of discovery had the objective of finding a shorter and less dangerous route to the riches of India, the Spice Islands and the Far East. The voyages of the Portuguese sailors centred on rounding Africa; in 1487 Bartholomew Diaz reached the Cape of Good Hope and in 1498 Vasco da Gama (1469–1524) landed in Calcutta and returned home some 26 months later. Similar voyages by the Spaniards followed the western route of Christopher Columbus, a Genoese sailor (1451–1506), and his ships the *Santa Maria*, *Pinta* and *Nina*. The Spaniards gradually colonised many of the islands in the Caribbean Sea and along the coastline adjacent to the West Indies. In the process Mexico was discovered, the isthmus of Panama was crossed and the Pacific Ocean reached. The discovery of the new continent of America was thus made, its name derived from the Florentine explorer, Amerigo Vespucci, who, when in the service of the Portuguese, first sighted the eastern seaboard of North America. The greatest voyage to the west, however, took place between 1519–1521 and was undertaken by Ferdinand Magellan (1480–1521), a Portuguese noble in the service of the Spanish king, Charles V. It is claimed that he based his project on an old map by Martin Behaim, which charted a possible route round South America in Antarctic latitudes. He sailed round South America with five well-equipped and well-armed ships; after crossing the Pacific Ocean he reached the Philippines, the object of his voyage, where he perished in an attack by the natives. The rest of his expedition came back to Seville on board one ship in August

1522. These and other voyages gave rise to the colonial empires of Portugal in Africa and eastern Asia and that of Spain in America and Asia (e.g. the Philippines).

Thus the harbours of the Iberian peninsula became the new centres of maritime trade, especially Lisbon in Portugal and the Spanish town of Seville. Antwerp was the trading centre on the coast of the North Sea.

The vessels used by the first 'conquistadores', as the Spanish conquerors and colonisers were called, were the caravels. Originally they were small, single-masted ships with lateen sail and were speedy and very manoeuvrable. The caravels of the sixteenth century were slender ships with two to three masts with lateen sails, one foremast with a square sail and a stern with an extended aftercastle. They were very fast and had a relatively small draught and a deadweight capacity of some 400 tons.

Smaller craft, such as the *Nina* and *Pinta* commanded by Columbus, also had lateen sails and their shape was reminiscent of the xebecs used by the Arabs in the Mediterranean. These were average sized vessels, with a fuller form, a main mast generally set with one square sail, possibly one topsail and a lateen sail on the mizzen mast; they were called 'naos'. Columbus' flagship, the *Santa Maria*, was a ship of this type.

Advances in shipbuilding kept pace with world trade expansion and were also stimulated by the numerous victories of the Knights of Rhodes and Malta over the pirates and the Turks and finally by the defeat of the Turkish navy off Lepanto in 1571 at the hands of the allied Christian fleet commanded by Don John of Austria. In the Mediterranean, within the Venetian sphere of influence, the prevailing type of warship was still the galley with one bank of oars and several oarsmen on each oar. It had three to four masts with lateen sails and a gun battery in the bow. The final phase of the development of the Mediterranean galley was reached with the galleass, which substituted a square bow with beak-head for the flat prolonged bow of the galley. The bow and stern were fitted with relatively low castles. Propulsion was by a single bank of oars, with two rowers to each oar; the three lateen sails remained constant. On both sides of the galleass there were gun batteries of up to 70 guns. They remained a feature of the French navy and that of the Italian City States until the eighteenth century.

The main type of merchant vessel in the second half of the fifteenth century and in the sixteenth century was the carrack, which began life in the Mediterranean, in the vicinity of the Venetian Republic and was adapted from the northern cog for long-distance travel. Carracks soon became the most common ships used by the Spanish colonists on their journeys to America. They were larger than the cogs; they had more decks and equal fore and sterncastles to accommodate a great number of passengers. Common features of most of the carracks were outer wales, strengthening the ship's skeleton on the outer side of the planking. Carracks mostly had three masts with two square sails on each, while the mizzen mast had a triangular lateen sail. From the middle of the fifteenth century even the short, inclined bowsprit, protruding from the bow, had a small square sail.

Carracks, however, were not simply merchant vessels. They were armed with several guns on either side of the main deck and in the sterncastle. These ships were regularly provided with lifeboats, situated amidships. Pulleys were in use for tightening the sails as the lanyards and deadeyes for shrouds. The anchors, which had arch-shaped flukes and a solid stock, were located one on each side. Because of their stability and improved navigation aids, carracks were introduced very quickly along the Atlantic seaboard and in the North Sea and were continually being improved upon. The square sails on the main and mizzen masts were supplemented by square topsails, which made the vessel more easily manoeuvrable.

Carracks were the predecessors of later, full-rigged ships and paved the way for the ultimate mastery of the seas. In this they were helped by the advancing frontier of navigational knowledge and by new instruments such as the cross-staff, a simple log for measuring the speed, and the hour glass, and by an increasing use of sea charts, although these as yet were very imperfect.

At this time England was not yet involved in the voyages of discovery. English merchants were embittered because their trade was restricted to the coastline of Europe, and their participation in the profitable commerce with the newly discovered Spanish and Portuguese territories in the Far East and America was prohibited by different decrees and charters. An exception to this general state of affairs was the voyage of discovery made by John Cabot and his three sons in the reign of Henry VII. Cabot sailed from England in search of Cathay in 1497, and reached instead the northern coast of America. The outcome of this voyage was the acquisition by England of Labrador, New Foundland and the coast of New England.

It was Henry VIII (1509—1547) who realised the importance of a good navy for the maintenance of his country's trade. Using carracks, by now a familiar craft along the Atlantic sea board, he built up his own navy at the beginning of the sixteenth century. He bought most of his ships but also built some. His flagship was the four-masted carrack, *Henry Grâce à Dieu*, built in 1514. Although Henry VIII is often considered the Father of the English Navy, he was too much concerned with domestic problems to pay much attention to voyages of discovery. During the reigns of his successors the voyages of English sailors were for the most part directed at finding a north-west passage to Cathay, especially after John Cabot had returned and proclaimed its existence.

A basic change in British maritime policy occurred in the reign of Elizabeth I (1558—1603). In the second half of the sixteenth century after years of trading and naval conflicts, mainly with Spanish ships, Elizabeth ordered the construction of a powerful fleet. She was supported by the greatest sailors of the day, among whom were Sir John Hawkins, later Treasurer of the Royal Navy, and Sir Francis Drake.

The backbone of this navy was the galleon, which was larger than the carrack and generally had three decks and three to four masts with square sails and one square sail on the bowsprit. Another feature of the galleon was the transom stern and attached sterncastle, which had several decks and galleries. The decoration of these castles and galleries became a display of the woodcarver's art, particularly in the stern where the officers were accommodated and where the commander had his quarters. Another feature of the galleon was the forehead, a sharp, pointed forecastle, which terminated in the slim projecting part under the bowsprit called the 'beak-head'. The beak-head was also carved and later carried a figurehead which illustrated the ship's name.

In 1588 Elizabeth's navy defeated the allied Spanish navy, the Armada, sent by Spain to take revenge for the forays of English corsairs in the Caribbean. The defeat of the Armada was caused largely by its lack of knowledge of the English coastal waters and by a storm during the return voyage. Only a half of the ships that set out returned safely to Spanish waters. Lord Howard of Effingham was the commander of the English fleet and his deputy, on board the *Revenge*, was Francis Drake, who started his career as one of Queen Elizabeth's corsairs. Between 1577—1580 Drake led an expedition of five ships round the world and returned after nearly three years in his ship the *Golden Hind* with tremendous booty. For his contribution to English seamanship, Francis Drake was later knighted.

After the defeat of the Armada the centre of activity in overseas trade and colonial expansion shifted to England. Famous sailors of this period included Sir Walter Ralegh, Sir Humphrey Gilbert, Captain John Smith and others. This period also saw the advent of the unfortunate yet remarkable slave trade which began in the second half of the sixteenth century and was initially sponsored by John Hawkins on board his ship, *Jesus of Lübeck*. Further voyages of discovery followed at short intervals, sponsored by different nations, as was the foundation of an increasing number of colonies. In 1620 the British 'Pilgrim Fathers', on board the *Mayflower*, which had a deadweight capacity of only 180 tons, reached the American coast off present-day Massachusetts and there they founded the first colony of Puritans in New England.

In 1600 the adventuresome English merchants founded the East India Company for trade with India and in so doing intensified English colonial expansion in that area. Galleons used in this trade became adapted for war at sea. Modifications included a slimmer shape, and the lowering and final disappearance of the forecastle to make way for the deck guns. The aftercastle was also lowered although the decoration and carving of its galleries continued to be luxurious. The fourth mast with the lateen sail disappeared. The number of square sails increased to some four to each mast, and the lateen sail only remained on the mizzen mast. A square sail was attached to the bowsprit. Sometimes a short mast was fixed at the end of the bowsprit and given yet another square sail. The number of decks and guns increased and in the course of the first half of the seventeenth century the galleon was converted into a three-masted warship with square sails and nearly one hundred guns. A typical representative of this period of development was the English three-decker, *Sovereign of the Seas*, which dates from 1637.

From among the states competing for a slice of the maritime trade, another contender emerged — Holland. For a long time the Dutch waged an unequal contest against the occupying Spanish troops, whilst at the same time attacking the Spanish galleons from their bases on the English coast. At the beginning of the seventeenth century a final separation of the northern Dutch protestant provinces from the rest of the Spanish Empire, was at last achieved. The first trading expeditions of the Dutch were directed northwards but after an unsuccessful expedition by their famous seaman, Barents, they turned towards the south. Using maps of the Portuguese voyages to India, the Dutch launched successful expeditions to that country at the end of the sixteenth century. They were similarly successful in sailing round South America via Cape Horn. In 1602 the Dutch merchants concerned with the India trade, joined together and founded the Dutch East India Company. As early as 1605 the Dutch were involved in their first maritime battle when they defeated the Spanish and Portuguese navies off Malacca. Gradually the Dutch squeezed the Portuguese out of the Indian trade and took their place. Thereafter Amsterdam succeeded Lisbon as the European centre for overseas trade.

The success of the Dutch overseas trade was less dependent on naval battles than on their merchant navy, which, in a relatively short time, outstripped those of the other European states. The basis of the Dutch fleet was a new type of merchantman, the Dutch fluyt. These ships were relatively long; their body had a full rounded shape at the water line; their sides sloped sharply inwards and their deck rose steeply towards the stern. Fluyts had three fairly tall masts with square, trapezoidal sails. They soon ploughed all the oceans of the world and were used as models by naval architects of other countries, especially Brandenburg, Venice and Russia. The Dutch became famous not only as excellent sailors and builders of ocean-going vessels but also as experts in river and coastal navigation. The shape of certain vessels with side floats (leeboards), used at this time for river navigation, has changed very little to this day. Holland was also the home of the yacht, which gradually spread as a sporting vessel, through the medium of the English court, round the world.

The commercial success which the Dutch merchants achieved, as a result of their monopolistic position, led in the second half of the seventeenth century to the Anglo-Dutch wars, which Holland initially dominated largely due to her excellent admirals, De Ruyter (1607—1676) and Tromp (1629—1691). In naval battles they employed a new fighting tactic, positioning their ships one behind the other, and in such manoeuvres the flagship of De Ruyter, the *De Zëven Provincien*, was most accomplished. Ultimately, however, the increasing strength of the British navy, built up under the guidance of the Secretary to the Admiralty, Samuel Pepys, in the reigns of Charles II and James II, led to the defeat of the Dutch navy, and their merchant marine withdrew from the European stage and concentrated its attention overseas. A perfect ship's shape of this period is provided by the sketches and engravings of such famous artists as the Dutchmen, Van De Velde, father and son, and the Czech, Hollar.

During the seventeenth century the first attempts at applying scientific principles to shipbuilding were made, at first only for warships. By the end of the sixteenth century English galleons were already being built by experienced specialists, although they did not yet work to fixed plans. The shape of a ship, in fact, could well change in the course of construction. Ships began to be built along really scientific lines in France during the time when Cardinal Richelieu and Colbert were the chief ministers; it was Louis XIV who founded the first training centre for naval architects. The first ship so produced was the *Couronne*, which had a displacement of about 2,000 tons and was built in 1638. Others quickly followed, including the *Soleil Royal*, the *Souverain* and the *Dauphin Royal*. Of these, the *Soleil Royal* was considered the most beautiful ship of the age because of her lavish decoration.

Thanks to ships built by these new methods and because of such excellent admirals as Tourville, Duquesne and others, France also became increasingly involved in overseas trade and in the colonisation of newly-discovered territories, largely in North America and Africa. Two Frenchmen concerned with the theories of shipbuilding, particularly the problems of stability and manoeuvrability, were the scientist, Bernouilli and the mathematician, Euler. The British continued to rely more on practical experience and empirical methods and did not found a school for shipbuilders at Portsmouth until 1811.

The Golden Age of Sailing Vessels

The period between the end of the seventeenth and the middle of the nineteenth centuries may be called the Golden Age of Sail. Ships became faster and larger and their hulls more slender. Timber was still the medium of construction. Ships now had a massive keel, a rib construction and their planking was butt-joined. The underwater parts of the hull were copper-plated. The main deck was gradually levelled; the tall fore-and-aft superstructures were lowered and the number of decks increased. The stern, initially circular, gradually acquired a transom shape, with an attached sterncastle and deck galleries. The bow had a long slim beak-head, which was slowly shortened. The number of sails increased, and the masts were commonly set not only with the main, topgallant and topsails, but also with royal sails. The square sail on the bowsprit disappeared and gave way to the focs set between the foremast and the bowsprit. The angle between the bowsprit and the main deck was reduced. The lateen sail on the mizzenmast was transformed into the gaff sail and top square sails were added. Rolling blocks were used to handle the sails. The rudder was controlled by a vertical steering wheel and a hand capstan was used for lowering the anchors. At the end of the seventeenth century the average deadweight capacity of such long-distance merchantmen was 400 tons and in exceptional cases 700 tons. During the first third of the eighteenth century it rose to 500 tons and by the end of the century it had risen to 1,200 tons, while in the first half of the nineteenth century ships designed for long voyages had a capacity of 1,500 tons.

The development of overseas trade with new parts of the world, especially North America and Asia, speeded up the evolution of new types of vessels. Thus on Asiatic routes, the East India companies developed special ships called East Indiamen, which were full-rigged with three masts, two or three decks and an extended sterncastle.

The difference was steadily decreasing between merchantmen and warships, whose design had changed during the course of the sixteenth century. Merchantmen now had more decks with rows of guns on each. The basic type of merchantman in the eighteenth century had become a full-rigged ship and barque.

In this period the classification of men-of-war began, based on the number of their guns. First line ships had approximately 100 guns, second line vessels had 80 guns and the most common third line ships had 50 guns, sometimes rising to 70. Warships of the fourth to sixth lines were usually small escort, patrol or blockade vessels. Fire power similarly increased and the perfect control of cannon and sails often decided the outcome of a battle. Britain in particular paid great attention to these arts. Well trained crews and expert commanders turned most naval encounters Britain's way in the eighteenth century. In this connection mention should be made of the battles with the Spanish navy in the Caribbean at the start of the century and against the French in the 1750s; battles which proved decisive in determining the settlement of North America. The most important took place at the end of the century when the Royal Navy under the command of such famous admirals as Howe, Hood, Jervis and Nelson defeated the enemy fleets of Spain and France and secured the mastery of the Atlantic and the Mediterranean for Great Britain.

This century saw many more great voyages of discovery. Among the most noteworthy were the voyage of the French captain, Bougainville, the three expeditions of Captain James Cook to the Pacific in the *Endeavour*, in 1768—70, the *Resolution* in 1772—75, and in the *Resolution* and *Discovery* in 1776—80, the voyage of the Dane, Vitus Bering (1681—1741) who, in the service of the Russians, searched for the north-west passage in 1728, and finally those expeditions of the Englishman, Hudson, and the Frenchman, Cartier, to the northern regions of America. The voyage of Captain Bligh in the *Bounty* to the Pacific Ocean and of G. Vancouver along the western seaboard of Canada, were similar exploratory enterprises. The success of such ventures was made possible by a greater understanding of astronomy and the use of such nautical instruments as the sextant, octant, log and chronometer and by the compilation and completion of sea maps. The construction of lighthouses, mainly along the western seaboard of Europe, also contributed to the improvements in navigation.

The Beginning of Steam Navigation

The first indication of the possibilities of a type of propulsion other than sail appeared in the middle of the eighteenth century. Early attempts at steam propulsion were carried out on inland waterways. As early as 1737 Jonathan Hulls experimented with a steam-driven, paddle-wheel barge that he intended to use to tug sailing ships. This attempt was unsuccessful but in 1783 the French Marquis, Jouffroy d'Abbans, successfully tested on the river Saône a paddle-wheel, steam-driven boat with a chain transmission, called the *Pyroscaphe*, which was powered by a double-acting, Watt steam engine. Official opposition made it impossible to develop further river steam navigation, although the vessel steamed upstream for fully fifteen minutes. In 1788, an engineer called William Symington and his associates, Miller and Taylor, were successful in trying out a small steam-propelled twin hull boat on a lake in the south of Scotland. For this venture a paddle wheel was placed between the hulls of the 25 foot vessel. A further experiment with a larger vessel failed and so it was not until 1802 that Symington succeeded in carrying out trials with an improved version, the *Charlotte Dundas*, on a canal between the Forth and the Clyde. This was powered by a single cylinder steam engine. Because of persistent opposition from canal owners, who feared damage to the banks, the introduction of steam propulsion was again postponed. In America the pioneer in this field was John Fitch. After successful trials in 1786 and 1788, he started a regular transport service in 1790 on the Delaware River using a paddle-wheel steamboat with a chain transmission. Despite this, John Fulton is generally considered the founder of steam navigation in America. In 1807 he opened a regular passenger transport service on the Hudson River from New York to Albany, using a paddle-wheel steamboat called the *Clermont*, driven by an English steam engine. Fulton went on to invent a submarine and in 1814 also built the first steam warship, *Demologos*.

Steam navigation on rivers soon followed in many parts of

Europe. In Glasgow, Scotland, in 1812, Henry Bell, using Fulton's patent, built a small paddle-wheel steamboat, the *Comet*, which was 51 feet (15.6 metres) long and was powered by a three horsepower engine.

Steam was first used at sea in 1819. The cargo sailing ship, *Savannah*, with a displacement of about 350 tons, and provided with paddle wheels and an auxiliary steam engine, steamed for about 85 hours during the crossing from America to Europe. The first voyage in the opposite direction, that is from the Old World to the New, took place in 1821 and was made by the first British steam warship, the *Rising Star*, a full-rigged, three-masted ship with a deadweight capacity of 428 tons. The ship had two paddle wheels placed in the hold and driven by a 70 horsepower steam engine. The first sea voyage using steam power throughout was made as late as 1827 by the paddle-wheeler, *Curaçao*, with gross tonnage 438 tons and a 100 h.p. engine. Carrying 57 passengers she travelled the distance between Rotterdam and Paramaribo in Dutch Guyana in 28 days at a speed of 6 knots.

In the following years the number of steamers and steam voyages increased. In 1821 the first all-iron steamer, *Aaron Manby*, was commissioned. In 1833 the Canadian paddle-steamer, *Royal William*, crossed the Atlantic in 25 days. She was owned by the Scotsman, Cunard, who founded a steamship company in 1840 for transporting passengers and mail between Liverpool and North America. In 1838 the steamer *Syrius*, closely followed by the *Great Western*, crossed the Atlantic from London to New York, steaming roughly along the present-day route of the North Atlantic companies. Shortly afterwards the *Great Western* started a regular service between Europe and America.

Almost at the same time as steam was first being used in ships, trials were being conducted with another propulsion system not dependent on paddle wheels. After unsuccessful or rather partially successful trials by the Englishman, Lyttelton, and the Americans, Fitch, Fulton and Stevens (whose projects were based either on Bernouilli or Bramah paddle wheels or on a spiral design, based on the Archimedean screw), Joseph Ressel (1793—1857) from landlocked Bohemia, succeeded in designing, positioning and testing a screw propeller. He conceived this idea probably as early as 1812 and after preliminary tests in Ljubljana on the river Krka in 1825 he carried out a successful trial of his screw propeller on board the *Civetta* at Trieste in 1829. His screw propeller, forming a part of the Archimedean screw, was placed aft in front of the rudder, which became standard practice from then on. Ressel did not use his invention, as the authorities seized on a defect in the steam engine as a pretext to cancel Ressel's licence to operate a service between Venice and Trieste. Soon after 1829, the date of Ressel's patent, one was also granted to the English businessman, Cummerow, for a very similar type of screw propeller. In 1832 a screw propeller was designed and patented by a French naval architect, Sauvage, and he is considered as its inventor in France. In May 1836 a further patent was taken out by the English farmer, Smith and also by John Ericsson, an engineer of Swedish origin, some six weeks later. Ericsson tested his screw propeller on two boats and used the second spectacularly to tug a 630-ton sailing ship at a speed of 5 miles an hour along the Thames. On the basis of similarly successful trials, Smith was commissioned by the British Admiralty in 1838 to build the ship, *Archimedes*, with a capacity of 237 tons and an engine of about 80 h.p. This first screw-propelled vessel steamed round the coasts of England and made a series of successful voyages. The first sea-going, screw-propelled, all-iron ship, the *Great Britain*, was built soon after, displacing some 3,618 tons and developing 1,014 h.p. She was built by I. K. Brunel who also designed the famous *Great Western*.

In the *Great Western* and the *Great Britain*, Brunel introduced such design innovations as watertight transverse bulkheads and an all-iron hull. The revolution in shipbuilding that took place in the nineteenth century was personified by his ship, the *Great Eastern*, originally named the *Leviathan*. Her dimensions and technical equipment were forty years ahead of her time. She was built completely of metal, provided with bulkheads and had a double bottom and sides. In addition to two side wheels, she had a screw propeller and was rigged with six masts. The ship was designed for passenger service between Europe, India and Australia. Paddle wheels were, however, unsuitable for such a great ship, as she rolled and pitched considerably and was finally withdrawn from passenger service and used for other purposes.

For some time paddle wheels and screw propellers were simultaneously employed in ships. After several decades, however, screw propulsion proved its worth and finally replaced paddle wheels altogether. One of the first trials to prove the advantages of the screw propeller over the paddle wheel, was the duel between the screw-propelled ship, *Rattler* and the paddle-steamer, *Alecto*; both were equipped with steam engines generating 200 h.p. Ultimately, in 1845 the *Rattler* triumphed, tugging the *Alecto* backwards, with her stern ahead, at a speed of nearly three knots. The last and best equipped paddle-steamer was the *Scotia*, owned by the Cunard company, built in 1861 and in service until 1875, during which time she cut the sailing time between Europe and North America down to nine days.

A Brief Survey of the Development of Warships in the Nineteenth Century

In the course of the nineteenth century steam and screw propulsion were adapted to the construction of warships. The hull planking, protected by sheets of metal, was gradually replaced by armour plating, while naval guns were mounted in fixed and later rotating turrets. The first warship with steam propulsion was the United States ship, the *Demologos*, built by Robert Fulton in 1814. From the middle of the nineteenth century iron and steel were used in building warships. Steam was now generally used in warships, although still in association with sail. Screw propulsion, however, was introduced very quickly, replacing the easily damaged paddle wheels. The bow ram, a typical feature of Mediterranean vessels, gradually disappeared as a feature of warships. The last significant battle using bow rams was fought by the Austrian, Admiral Tegetthoff, against the Italian navy off Vis in the Adriatic in 1866.

The French naval architect, Dupuy de Lôme, who built the experimental 5,000-ton, screw-propelled vessel, *Napoleon*, in 1852, is usually considered the inventor of armoured warships. His other ship was the first armoured frigate, *La Gloire*, which was launched in 1859. *La Gloire* signalled the demise of sailing men-of-war. The construction of all-iron warships was quickly tackled by England, where the all-iron frigates, *Warrior* and *Black Prince*, were launched in 1861. Frigates, which were a type of small, slender yet speedy sailing ship, were also developed in France; these had a single row of guns on deck and proved useful for coast guard duties. Again, on frigates, sails were gradually replaced by steam.

The first armoured steamships soon proved their worth; a case in point was the engagement during the American Civil War between the *Merrimac*, owned by the Confederates and the *Monitor*, owned by the Federalists. The *Monitor*, built by the inventor of the screw propeller, Ericsson, was equipped with a rotating turret, which bristled with naval guns. This war showed that wooden warships had reached the limit of their development. Revolving turrets with the biggest guns were generally placed along the central axis of the vessel to ensure the maximum possible radius of fire around the ship. The techniques of sea warfare continued to improve. The torpedo and mine were invented and the first successful trials with submarines were carried out. The first torpedoes were not self-propelled; they were merely mines attached to a long rod with which a ship struck the sides of an enemy vessel. Later compressed air was used to drive the torpedoes and they became the main weapon of submarines.

The development of submarines started with the unsuccessful

experiments of the Dutchman, Van Drebell, in 1625, followed by the Englishman, Day, in 1770 and leading to the ball-shaped, wooden submarine, *Turtle*, built by David Bushnell for intervention in the War of American Independence in 1776. About 1800 Robert Fulton developed this new weapon further and called his submarine *Nautilus*. Fulton's work and experiments were not totally unsuccessful but he failed to interest the authorities in his invention. However in the middle of the nineteenth century successful trials with submarines were carried out by the German, Wilhelm Bauer, who devoted his whole life to this project. He did not live to see either the ultimate practical application or reap the benefit of his work. An effective means of propulsion was the main problem for a long time. Preliminary attempts tried manual and later steam propulsion methods and it was only in the 1870s that the Russian inventor, Drzewicki, used accumulator batteries. The first serviceable submarines, built to designs by the Frenchman, Gustave Zédé and the American, Holland, were finally constructed at the end of the nineteenth century.

By the beginning of the twentieth century the following main types of warship were in use:

Battleship:
Maximum displacement up to 15,000 tons. Armed with 30.5-cm guns.

Battle cruiser:
Warship with a smaller number of lower calibre guns, weaker armouring, yet faster speed; used in sea battles and for attacking coastal targets.

Light and armoured cruiser:
Fast warship with less powerful equipment and armouring, used for the protection of merchantmen.

Destroyer
Small, fast warship with lower firing power, equipped with torpedoes and depth charges; used to engage submarines, to attack enemy vessels and to protect convoys.

Submarine:
Underwater craft, equipped with torpedoes and occasionally one gun; used to destroy large warships and merchantmen.

In addition to the above, there were other vessels adapted for special purposes, such as torpedo boats, minelayers and minesweepers; all of which appeared at this time.

The Development of Steam Power at Sea

The second half of the nineteenth century was characterised by a tremendous increase in the volume of sea traffic, particularly in the Atlantic Ocean, which saw a continual flow of European emigrants to North America after the end of the Napoleonic Wars. Similarly the Southern Atlantic, the Indian and Pacific Oceans were the scene of intensive activity. Steam was the dominant means of propulsion, and the ship's casing was made of rivetted iron plates. The size of ships was also increasing, as was the output of their engines. Sails, however, did not entirely disappear from the high seas. The beginning of the second half of the century saw the advent of the glorious age of the clippers. These were fast, generally three-masted, full-rigged ships with square sails. They had a slender shape and superb sailing qualities. Clippers originated in America and soon were also used by European shipowners for speedy passenger and cargo services; the transport of tea from India and China to Europe and passengers to America and Australia, and later on other goods such as wool was undertaken by the clipper ship. Thanks to their shape, rigging and the experience of their captains, clippers could reach speeds of up to 21 knots on their record-breaking voyages. The construction of the Suez Canal, however, dealt them a fatal blow. The inheritors of their lost glory were the multi-masted, sailing cargo ships at the dawn of the twentieth century, which had full or fore-and-aft rigging. They were involved in the bulk cargo trade, carrying goods such as cereals, coal and saltpetre. Some of them are still sailing the oceans of the world, although at present the glorious age of sea-going, sailing ships is largely recalled by the training vessels of the merchant and naval services of a few maritime nations.

During the period when relatively slow cargo steamers were being built for freight transport, shipping companies competed against one another in building larger, faster and more luxurious steamers. They included the Cunard Steamship Co., a later English company the White Star Line, the British India Steam Navigation Company and the German companies, Hamburg-America and Norddeutscher Lloyd. In 1840 the gross tonnage of Cunard's first wooden, paddle-wheel steamers was 1,150 tons, whilst the power of their engines did not exceed 740 h.p.; in 1892 the gross tonnage of the same company's ships, the *Campania* and *Lucania* reached 13,000 tons with 26,000 h.p. engines. The giant ships made in Britain and Germany alternated in capturing the speed record on Atlantic routes and at the beginning of the twentieth century this accolade, the so-called Blue Ribbon of the Atlantic, was won by the Cunard line's ship, the *Mauretania*, with an approximate gross tonnage of 35,600 tons and with steam turbines generating 70,000 h.p. The *Mauretania* kept the record until 1929. The tragic sinking of the luxurious S.S. *Titanic* in 1912 happened because her captain wished to reach New York in daylight and underestimated the danger of floating icebergs. The Blue Ribbon was not at stake as the *Titanic* was a far less powerful ship than the holder of the record, the *Mauretania*. This catastrophe, followed by the First World War, damped down the competitive spirit of the great companies and encouraged rigorous surveys by the various Classification Societies during the construction of ships. Other safety measures included the setting up of an iceberg survey service, the introduction of wireless telegraphy and the conclusion of the First

Convention on the Safety of Life at Sea (SOLAS). The beginning of the twentieth century also saw the advent of the internal combustion engine, in the English tanker, *Vulcanus*, in 1910 and in the Danish cargo ship, *Selandia*, in 1912. The mechanical propulsion of ships by internal combustion engines, particularly fuel oil, diesel engines, was gradually introduced in cargo vessels and smaller warships, especially submarines. At present more than half of the world's ship tonnage is equipped with diesel marine engines of various designs, among which the best known are Burmeister-Wain, Sulzer, M.A.N., Fiat, Gotawerken and Hitachi, which generate up to 28,000 h.p.

The greatest builder of sea-going ships from the eighteenth century onwards was Great Britain, who, until the Second World War, had the greatest merchant and naval fleet. Since then, Germany, France, Japan and the U.S.A. have kept pace with or surpassed Britain. Only the great industrial powers could afford to construct large passenger ships to compete for the Blue Ribbon. As a result, in the period between 1928 and 1938 Germany *(Bremen* 1929, 1933*)*, Great Britain *(Queen Mary* 1936, 1938*)*, France *(Normandie* 1935, 1937*)*, and Italy *(Rex* 1933*)* alternated in holding this trophy. These ships were of a considerable size, were very powerful and reduced the time for crossing between Europe and America to less than five days, although their operation was expensive as they were driven by steam turbines and fuelled by heavy oils. They had screw propellers and were rivetted, although by the thirties smaller craft were being welded. Cargo ships were specified according to the nature of their freight; for example general cargoes (bulk carriers), liquid cargoes (tankers). Passenger ships increased in size and acquired more sophisticated technical equipment, while safety devices were continually being improved. In this period, the shipyard for building sea-going vessels became a huge factory employing thousands of workers and a place where not only ship's hulls were built, but also ship's machinery, propellers and all types of deck machinery. A series of specialised companies came into existence to outfit ships. The construction of a ship was now based on scientific research that tried to decide the best shape of the ship's hull, the various systems of ship's propulsion and considered the manoeuvrability of the craft. Ships were repaired in special dry or floating docks which, when the water was pumped out, gave free access to the ship's hull.

The Development of Ships after the Second World War

The Second World War, like all previous wars, contributed to the development of navigation and shipbuilding. Improvements in production technology made it technically possible to build forever bigger and more reliable cargo, passenger and special vessels. Currently, the largest cargo ships are the tankers built in Japan and used to carry oil from the Persian Gulf to Japan and Europe. These ships are already so large that they cannot sail through the Suez Canal and must go round South Africa. Their operation is fully automatic and requires only several dozen expertly trained crew members. At present the size record is held by the giant tanker of the Tokyo Tanker Co., the *Nisseki Maru*, which has a deadweight of 372,400 tons. The average size of other tankers varies from 60,000 to 80,000 tons, while conventional cargo ships are built with a gross tonnage of 20,000 to 30,000 tons. The average speed of such cargo ships, which before the Second World War was 12 to 13 knots, has increased to 18 knots.

The building of cargo vessels has become further specialised according to the type of freight. Thus special ships are built for transporting fruit, minerals, liquid gas, wine, cellulose, motor cars, containers and barge type containers. Cargo ships conveying containers and vehicles are designed for continual loading and unloading. They are called roll-on roll-off ships.

The construction of passenger ships has continued to develop. The largest ship is the *France*, which until recently was the most up-to-date and the newest. Now, however, the newest passenger ship is the *Queen Elizabeth II*, which was launched in October 1968. The holder of the Blue Ribbon since 1952 has been the

American ship, the *United States*, which has a gross tonnage of 53,329 tons and which has reached the speed of 35.6 knots. The light alloys and plastics have been used to a great extent in the construction of these passenger ships and have naturally also been applied on a large scale in the construction of other types of ship. The above-mentioned passenger ships are, however, of exceptional size. The average passenger ship has a length of about 200 metres, a displacement of 20,000 to 30,000 tons and can carry 1,000 to 1,300 passengers at a speed of around 25 knots. They are more economic to operate than the larger ships. The British *Northern Star* and *Southern Cross*, the Italian *Leonardo da Vinci*, *Galileo Galilei* and *Michelangelo* and the Dutch *Statendam* are representative of such ships. Recently special passenger vessels have been built for cruising in different regions. They are equipped for a smaller number of passengers in one class and for long periods at sea. Their gross tonnage is around 25,000 tons and their speed approximately 20 knots. The latest of them are the German *Hamburg*, the Swedish *Kungsholm*, and the Norwegian *Sea Venture* and *Island Venture*.

The majority of sea-going ships are driven by internal combustion engines. Large craft such as passenger ships are equipped with steam turbines and oil heating. Gradually, although slowly, nuclear power is making headway as a means of propulsion, particularly for warships. Following a series of American and Soviet submarines and other naval craft, such as the aircraft carrier *Enterprise* and missile cruisers, the Soviet icebreaker *Lenin* was provided with nuclear power in 1959. In 1962 the American nuclear ship *Savannah* was put into service for a trial period to carry passengers and cargo. The construction of other nuclear-powered ships was completed in Germany (the *Otto Hahn*) and in Japan (the *Mutsu*). Despite this, in smaller craft used mainly for military purposes, the gas turbine of up to 8,000 h.p. is increasingly preferred as the propulsion unit.

Research into hydrodynamics has led to new boat designs. Wing boats, or hydrofoils, of various sizes have been successfully tried out both on rivers and at sea. After reaching a certain speed their hull rises out of the water because of the hydrodynamic lift of foils located under it. The average speed of these craft is 70 to 75 km per hour, although the top speed of special military vessels can be as high as 130 km per hour. Another novelty are hovercraft, which create, by means of a system of fans, an air cushion between the surface of the water and the bottom of the craft, thus reducing frictional resistance and achieving a higher speed. The forward thrust is effected by air propellers. They can reach a speed of 100 km per hour. The hydrofoil and hovercraft are used for short-distance, passenger and cargo transport across channels and straits. Hydrofoils have even been used in the U.S.S.R. on long stretches of rivers.

The safety of ships is secured by the use of radar and echo-sounders, whilst the ship's engines and deck machinery are operated by remote control. Automatic steering gear or the gyropilot similarly simplifies the work of the deck officers. Non-inflammable materials are extensively used for interior furnishings; automatic fire extinguishers, operated by remote control, are usually installed. The roll and pitch of ships, especially of passenger vessels, may be reduced by using various types of stabilisers. The safety of passengers and crew has also been increased by the introduction of unsinkable lifeboats and self-inflatable, roofed rafts.

Continuing research into all aspects of shipbuilding is reflected in the application of multi-bladed screw propellers, propellers with adjustable blades, the streamlining of bows and sterns, revolving propeller nozzles, self-steering gear and various other steering devices which help large ships to enter harbours and manoeuvre amongst a number of other craft and in difficult areas of waterways.

New systems of sea and river transport are gradually being tested and introduced. For example, on the great European and American rivers, the pushing of barges and the towing of plastic floating containers carrying liquid, is being used, and submarine navigation is also being tested as a possible mode of transport.

Sailing and motor boating is increasingly becoming a favourite sport among a broad section of the population.

New types of vessels continue to be developed for special purposes: ships to carry cars, special types of fishing boats, factory ships for processing fish at sea and modern, efficient floating dredgers and cranes. To exploit the resources of the seabed, drilling and mining ships and floating, drilling platforms are being used. Great attention is paid to maritime research and exploration of the seabed, involving the use of research ships and special submarines.

Ships are now built in great sections and blocks, with partly installed machinery and piping systems. Shipbuilding today is carried out under the permanent observation of Classification Societies whose rules ensure a high degree of reliability of design and operation. Sea and river navigation are governed by international agreements and conventions, whose rules cover all aspects of shipping. Such measures are essential because of the continuing increase in the number of ships sailing the oceans of the world. The total deadweight capacity of all ships reached 268 million tons in 1972. The first five positions in the world's ship-owning league are held by the fleets flying the flags of Liberia, Japan, Great Britain, Norway and the U.S.S.R.

There have been similar developments in warships. Even in the First World War several maritime encounters took place that were comparable to the sea battles of many years ago, although later naval operations were limited to submarine warfare, the protection of merchant convoys and the tracking down of auxiliary cruisers or armoured merchantmen. Large warships only intervened in certain individual cases. By the end of the First World War the importance of air power in the navy was recognised and was confirmed during the Second World War, when the war at sea was decided by several battles involving aircraft carriers. As a result, after the Second World War a fundamental re-evaluation of the role of fleets and naval tactics took place, the outcome of which was the abandonment of large warships, such as battleships, battle cruisers and heavy cruisers. The great naval powers paid more attention to building submarines with a greater range, to the construction of aircraft carriers and missile cruisers and to the special redesigning of smaller craft such as light cruisers, destroyers and frigates for anti-submarine and anti-air raid defence. The modern equipment of warships consists in the main of defence weapons against submarines, aircraft and missiles and involves a high degree of automation, both of the ship's control and armament.

THE CONSTRUCTION OF A SHIP

SHIPS AS WATER CRAFT

At first sight no particular difference is apparent in these two expressions. 'Craft' is a broad term, covering every floating body used for service on the water; thus not only ships but also boats, floating-dredgers, rafts and other vessels are included no matter what their function, be it industrial or transportation. On the other hand, 'ship' is a narrower notion, indicating a steerable, hollow craft, which transports passengers or cargo or both, or serves for other purposes. There is also a distinction between the terms 'ship' and 'boat'. By 'boat' is generally understood a small craft for sporting, pleasure and fishing purposes or, in the case of lifeboats, a craft to be used on large ships. Exceptions to this rule, however, can be found in the use of the word 'boat' in the terms 'patrol boat', 'lifeboat', 'ferryboat', 'steamboat' and 'tugboat', since their size is closer to that of a ship than a boat.

Ships, boats and other craft must be of the appropriate size, shape, structure and have the requisite drive and equipment to fulfil the purpose designed for them. Shipbuilding has developed over thousands of years, from craft made by hand to the factory and industrial production of large sea-going and river vessels.

The construction and design of ships has become both an art and a science. The ship's architect designs his vessel on the basis of previous research and his own experience, and a regard for all factors determining the nature of the craft: its purpose, navigation zone, type of propulsion, materials used etc. Individual construction of ships and boats by hand has survived only among amateur sportsmen, fishermen and primitive peoples in all parts of the world, who build according to the experience of their ancestors.

CONSTRUCTION

A ship is generally composed of two main sections: the hull and the superstructure. Superstructures may be of different sizes and variously located on board the ship. They may extend from one side to the other or be separated from the sides of the ship by gangways. In smaller vessels or when the height of the ship is limited, as with river craft because of bridges, these superstructures may be semi-sunken or be simple shelters, steering houses or sunken cabins, as in yachts. Certain types of ships have their superstructures in a particular place and can be distinguished accordingly. Tankers and container ships have a superstructure aft, Great Lakes ships have one aft and another, the bridge, fore, whilst tugboats have a forward one.

The hull of a ship consists of its skeleton, which is encased on top by the deck and at the sides and bottom by the shell. The hull and the superstructures may be horizontally subdivided by several decks. The continuous watertight deck used usually for calculating resistance is called the main deck. The decks over the main deck have their own names: upper, boat, promenade, and shelter deck. According to the construction and extent of the decks it is possible to distinguish various types of ships, for example those with shelter decks, spar decks and aftercastles.

The skeleton of a ship is a system of basic structural longitudinal and transverse members, the purpose of which is to provide the craft with sufficient strength. The main structural member of the skeleton, situated along the bottom central line, is the central keelson or vertical keel. At the bow the keelson merges into the stem and in the stern the sternpost. The sternpost is usually adapted to take the rudder shaft. In one-screw ships it has a hole in it for the propeller shaft. Certain smaller vessels have their stern finished by a vertical or oblique surface called the transom, the origin of which is to be found in medieval carracks. According to the shape of the posts, which indicate the form of the stern and bow, different types of bow can be distinguished, such as the lean bow, the bold bow, the spoon bow, the flared bow and the bulbous bow. Types of stern include the elliptical, the transom and the cruiser stern. In addition to the central keelson, the ship's bottom may also have side keelsons, which increase its longitudinal strength. The lowest part of the ship's bottom is the keel. The bottom of river vessels is usually flat, whereas in sea-going ships it has some deadrise. The larger the deadrise angle, the better the stability and manoeuvrability of the ship. For this reason sea-going sailing vessels and yachts have deeper keels than normal ships. For this purpose the hull of yachts is extended downwards to form a powerful keel. The submerged parts of large passenger ships used to have fins, or stabilisers, which could be extended outwards and revolved, to reduce the pitch and roll of the ship.

To increase their longitudinal strength, larger craft have a double bottom, which is covered from above by continuous plating, in other words the deck, and transversely subdivided by floors into watertight sections called cofferdams. The other longitudinal, structural parts are the side stringers, located on the hull sides and the longitudinal deck beams which support the deck.

The frames are the main transverse members of the ship's hull. They are connected to the floors on the bottom and to the deck beams on the deck. The decks are made of metal plates or wooden planks or some similar material and are attached to deck beams and girders. The decks are either continuous or partially open, that is punctuated by cargo hatchways, openings and casings.

Other important structural parts of the hull are the transverse bulkheads attached to the frames, usually watertight and subdividing the hull into compartments. These watertight sections are important for the transverse strength and buoyancy of the craft. In large ships, longitudinal bulkheads are also erected in the hull, especially in those used to transport bulk and liquid cargoes, to prevent the cargo shifting during the voyage and affecting the ship's stability.

The shell of the ship is fixed to the frames, bulkheads, side stringers, decks and to the framing of the ship's bottom. Steel plates are used for the shell in nearly all greater ships. Formerly they were overlapped for rivetting but at present they are buttwelded. The ships of earlier centuries were planked, which meant that the individual planks either overlapped each other rather like tiles (this was known as the clinker-built system and was used in Viking ships and cogs), or they were butt-joined by the carvel system, used for the majority of wooden vessels. The other wooden parts of the skeleton, such as the frames and posts, were assembled from smaller pieces into a large whole or were bent into shape. Naturally shaped parts of branches and logs were also used. Such wooden parts were connected by pins, wedges, nails, battens and later by rivets and bolts. The wooden planking was sheathed in lead or copper plates to prevent sea animals and plants fouling the hull.

The skeleton of the ship's superstructure is similar to that of the hull as it also consists of longitudinal and transverse structural members, sheathed in metal or some other material.

Timber is the classical material for building ships. Mild iron came into use in the nineteenth century and later steel was employed. After the Second World War light alloys were used, particularly in the construction of the superstructure, and plastics or reinforced fibre glass are used in the building of smaller craft. Besides plastics, linen or textile reinforced rubber is now used as the shell for sporting-boats and inflatable rafts.

Wood and plywood remain the classical material for yachts, especially such woods as cedar, oak, mahogany and teak.

SHIP'S PROPULSION

The oldest method of propelling a vessel is the power generated by the human hand. The Ancient Egyptians propelled their craft by paddling in a standing position and later by rowing in a standing or sitting position. The Phoenicians and the Assyrians similarly used oar propulsion but their oarsmen were in a sitting position. In fact human energy was employed to drive Greek, Roman and medieval galleys up to the end of the eighteenth century.

Almost at the same time as the use of oars, wind power began to be harnessed as a means of propulsion. The first sails were square and stretched between two yards, although later they were suspended from only one upper yard. The sail was furled at first by lowering the upper yard, then by reducing its area by folding it like a Venetian blind and later by shortening it by means of reefing points. For a long time one mainsail was thought to be sufficient. Only in the first century BC was another square sail added to an inclined mast (artemon) in the bow. This was followed by a tringular top sail on the main mast. The lateen triangular sail was most probably of Arabic origin and was used in Byzantine times. In the Middle Ages the square sail of northern origin came into use. Both types of sail were employed for the first time in naos and carracks, though the use of more masts was already commonplace. In the second half of the fifteenth century another small square sail was added, which increased in size in the course of the sixteenth century and was set on the main and later on the foremast of the carracks. In galleons these sails developed into a set of square sails, the basis of later full-rigging. A more advanced form of rigging could be seen on the fluyts and soon after on the full-rigged ship of the seventeenth and eighteenth centuries. Thereafter rigging continued to improve and a series of different types of sailing ship made their appearance, characterised by the use of square sails and fore-and-aft ones. The swan song of sailing ships was the age of the clippers in the nineteenth century and of the great sailing ships at the dawn of the twentieth. Currently sail is only used for training ships, sports yachts, fishing boats and tribal craft.

The use of steam and the invention of the steam engine revolutionised ship's propulsion. From the first attempts with paddlewheel drive at the end of the eighteenth century, the progress towards its implementation can be approximately traced to the period between 1820 and 1860. During the 1840s, however, a more efficient and simpler propulsion device was introduced, namely the screw propeller, which has been retained to the present day. Paddle wheels gave a satisfactory efficiency particularly in shallower waters and survived in river craft for a long time. Not until the middle of the twentieth century did certain types of vessel, particularly restricted river craft, change over to other propulsion devices, such as the Voith-Schneider vertical blade propeller, the water jet or pump propulsion for shallows and variously modified screw propulsion techniques, such as the Kort nozzle, Z-propulsion and the Harbour-Master with its tilting screw propeller shaft.

The piston steam engine maintained its primacy well into this century, although before the First World War the steam turbine took over the running and has remained the most suitable propulsion for such powerful ships as passenger liners, battleships and giant tankers. In the course of the First World War and increasingly afterwards, internal combustion engines, mainly diesel engines, directly connected to the ship's propeller, were gradually introduced, and are currently used in large cargo ships and tankers. After the Second World War gas turbines, generating up to 8,000 h.p., were employed but only in smaller, especially naval craft. Other types of propulsion such as ones using electric batteries or trolleys have subsequently been tried out but only in small craft in controlled conditions.

The ship's engines are located in the machinery and boiler

rooms, which are separated from the other parts of the ship by watertight bulkheads. During the age of steam-driven ships, large boiler rooms were built for stoking coal into the furnaces of steam boilers, at first by hand and later mechanically. Today coal heating has been replaced by oil (fired) heating, which uses automatically-controlled oil burners. After the Second World War the use of nuclear fuel for steam production was considered, especially for naval vessels. Nuclear fuel, because of the tiny consumption of the reactors, is definitely the fuel of the future. Piston steam engines on ships have also undergone a long process of development from side-lever engines to the horizontal, compound multiphase engines of the twentieth century. Modern steam turbines are efficient, responsive high pressure engines, running at high temperatures and fully automatic. Internal combustion engines in use at the beginning of the twentieth century generated several tens of h.p. on each cylinder, today 3,000 to 4,000 h.p. on each cylinder.

They are used as slow revolving engines, directly connected to the screw propeller, or as medium-speed engines with reduction and reverse gear boxes. Alongside the main engines, pumps, ship's piping systems and appropriate control mechanisms are installed in the engine room, ensuring a supply of fuel, cooling oil and water, the production of compressed air to start the engines and the discharge of exhaust gases. Recently, the aim of naval architects has been to promote such a degree of automatic control over the ship's engine room that the presence of crew members there could be dispensed with.

The propeller shaft is driven by the main engine directly from the engine room and is led through the propeller shaft tunnel. In some ships propulsion is not direct but transmitted by generators and electric motors, which drive the shortened propeller shaft in the aft section of the ship. Most cargo ships have a single propeller, because of their simple design; more screw propellers are used in passenger ships and special craft. The maximum number of screw propeller blades is seven; the largest screw propeller so far produced with fixed blades had a diameter of

26.9 feet, whereas the greatest one with adjustable blades had a diameter of 18.3 feet. The greatest power, anything from 160,000 to 200,000 h.p., can be found in warships, aircraft carriers and passenger liners.

DECK MACHINERY

One of the most important pieces of deck machinery aboard ship is the anchor equipment. Anchors have undergone a very interesting development, progressing from the stone and wooden anchors with iron arms of Ancient History to simple metal anchors with a solid stock, through admiralty anchors of old-fashioned type, to various patent stockless anchors with folding arms having greater holding power. Machinery for raising and lowering anchors has seen a similar development. Originally anchors were simply thrown into the water and raised by hand. When heavier anchors became necessary, tackle blocks and the anchor davit were used, and later manual capstans with vertical shafts. When steam came into use, it was applied to the anchor and windlass capstans. Instead of ropes, chains came to be used. Today, electricity or diesel engines are used for smaller windlasses and capstans, while larger ships have hydraulic or electro-hydraulic machinery.

The steering equipment, the second most important item of deck machinery has progressed in a similar way. From steering oars at the sides of vessels, which were loosely suspended or fixed on a pivot, as in Viking ships, and provided with a single hand tiller, there developed the stern rudder with a whipstaff and then control by a hand wheel in a horizontal and later in a vertical position. Transmission to the rudder shaft was by means of cables, chains and the steering quadrant. Today the steering mechanism is generally fully powered. Powerful steering engines are used to turn the rudder blade and are located in the steering room. The engines are mainly electrohydraulically driven and remote-controlled from the steering column in the wheel house. Recently even this aspect of the steering of the ship has been made fully automatic. The automatic steering unit, or gyropilot, steers the ship according to given navigational data and the ship's commander needs only check the correct operation of this complicated apparatus. To improve the manoeuvrability of ships such as liners, ferries and icebreakers, in harbour and other restricted places, various additional devices are used built into the bow, such as a V.S. propeller or a bow jet propeller.

Lifeboats and working boats were found on board ship at a relatively early date; even Roman merchantmen had them. They are lowered to the water by means of davits and purchases. The design of the davits was modernised in the nineteenth and twentieth centuries when the lowering of boats to the water became mechanised. Now various types of davits, such as roundbar davits, collapsible or quadrantal davits and the latest gravity davits, which slide over the water, bring such boats from the deck and lower them. Boat davits and their winches are generally electrically driven. Recently, covered boats that do not capsize or sink have been widely introduced. They are sometimes partly replaced by solid or self-inflatable rafts which offer more protection against the effect of the weather and are safer than lifeboats of normal type.

Mooring equipment is a further important item of deck machinery. It consists of a set of bollards, fairleaders and cleats which guide the cables when the craft is being towed or moored to a harbour pier or anchoring buoys.

In earlier times masts were habitually used for setting sails but now, when ships have other types of propulsion, masts are used for radio and telegraphic aerials, to carry signal and position lights, radar scanners and flag signals.

Depending on their destination, craft may also be equipped with other types of deck equipment. Merchantmen are fitted out with their own cargo-handling machinery, unless harbour equipment is used for loading and unloading goods. Such machinery includes cargo derricks and booms, which are usually inclined and revolvable and fixed to various types of cargo masts.

They have their own electrically or hydraulically driven cargo winches, which, by means of a system of rollers, control the runners, guys, hooks, grabs and other devices. Ships used for towing other craft are fitted with the necessary towing equipment. Usually a towing hook is the main piece of such equipment and possibly an electrically or otherwise powered towing winch, particularly on rivers. Tugs tow the great sea ships to their moorings at the quayside and they are also used to tow river barges and lighters. Pushing is a modern method of river transport and is increasingly used on inland waterways. The pusher-tug has pushing poles and coupling winches, the purpose of which is to join firmly the pushed barge or a whole set of barges to the pushing tug.

SHIP'S PIPE SYSTEMS AND ELECTRICAL POWER PLANT

To ensure the safe operation of ships and create comfortable conditions for the daily life of crew and passengers on board, vessels are equipped with a complex system of pumps and pipes. The pipe systems which are vital to the safety of the ship are the drainage and salvage piping which pump out any water that might have penetrated the ship's interior. Further crucial pipe systems include the fire piping, which gives warning of and extinguishes fires, and the ballast piping. By means of ventilation heads and fans, the ventilation ducts allow a sufficient flow of air through the ship. They are part of the air-conditioning and central heating system. The water pipes connected to the ship's water tanks, supply the ship with fresh and general purpose water. The sanitary water and sewage pipes drain off waste. Distillation plant for the production of fresh water from sea water is found in most modern ships. The ship's pipe systems also ensure the automatic provision of water and other supplies in the galleys, storerooms, refrigerators, showers, bathrooms etc. Another important device onboard the ship is the electrical system, the operation of which is ensured by means of electricity produced by the ship power plant. To supply ships with electric power auxilliary aggregates, running independently of the main engines, are usually used. Generators driven by the main propulsion engines are rarely used for this purpose. Storage batteries are kept to provide emergency supplies for some important devices and systems (emergency lighting, signalization). The system of electrical equipment includes the power devices for the drive of deck machinery, lighting and telecommunication devices (radio, telephone) and navigation equipment (echograph, compass, radar).

THE SHIP'S OUTFIT AND ACCESSORIES

The outfitting of a ship includes the provision of the side scuttles and deadlights, windows, doors, companionways, hatches, skylights and covers, stairs, ladders, rails, bulwarks and portholes, wave breakers, floors and gratings etc.

The interior fittings include the cabin furniture, service room and other room furnishings. The inventory is an important ship's accessory, as is the supply of spare parts that every ship should hold in reserve. Inventories include the deck inventory and the life-saving appliances, which contains life-saving rings, collars, jackets and preservers. Again, the navigational inventory gives details of nautical instruments, maps, flags etc., while the emergency inventory caters for anything that might be needed after a collision. The engine room inventory details spares for the repair of the ship's machinery, and the workshop inventory contains general repair supplies.

NAVIGATION

In ancient times the navigation of a vessel depended on the experience of the master. Gradually various aids were added to help the captain in this responsible work. For many centuries seamen had to rely on a knowledge of the coasts and basic astronomy and it was a long time before they left the coastal waters and ventured out on to the open sea. Thus proper sea voyages began only in Viking times, around AD 1000. Then came the discovery of the compass and hour glasses, and the use of the astrolabe, cross staff, log and finally the sextant, all of which were crucial to the voyages of discovery. In addition to written navigation instructions, which seem to have been possessed by early sailors, imperfect maps were in use at the dawn of the New Age. Techniques developed in the eighteenth and nineteenth centuries provided for near-perfect navigation, even on long ocean voyages, though risks continued to be great. Even today when excellent navigation aids supply the master with continuous bearings giving his ship's geographical position, data of speed, depth, exact time and meteorological and radar information, collisions still occur, fires break out, ships run aground and sinkings cause loss of human life and valuable cargo. It is indeed surprising how many ships are lost every year, despite perfect communication between bridge and engine room by means of telegraph, telephone and the automatic transmission of orders and data; despite the ever increasing perfection of steering and navigation equipment, such as gyropilots, radars, radiolocators and remote-control systems; despite perfect radio and telegraphic communication, despite the safety and watch services at sea, excellent maps and charts, lighthouses, radio sending stations, lightships and coastguard signals. The causes of such losses include derelictions of duty by officers and crew, imperfect design and construction of a vessel or mistaken evaluation of communications data; and the unpredictable power of the sea and nature, which man has tried to master for over a thousand years of sailing history.

It lies, however, within human power to cut down the losses caused by the first and second causes. Shipyards design and build ships using the most up-to-date methods of production technology and applying experience from other branches of industry. Similarly sailors pass on the experience they gain from handling such ships to the builders and try to ensure the safety of shipping through international conventions, design and navigation rules and regulations. Care is also taken in the training of crews and the appointment of experienced men as the masters of ships. All this confirms the truth of the old proverb: 'Navigare necesse est, vivere non est necesse'.

TABLE I

A cross-section of a merchantman of the middle of the sixteenth century

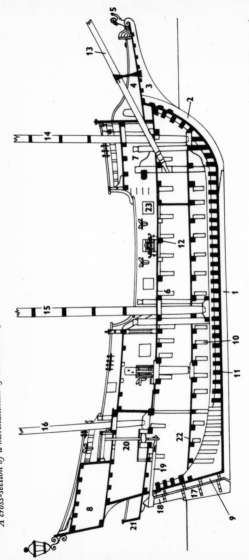

1 Keel, 2 Sternpost, 3 Beak-head, 4 The beak-head deck, 5 The figure-head, 6 Main deck, 7 Forecastle, 8 Aftercastle, 9 Sternpost, 10 Frames, 11 Floors, 12 Deck beams, 13 Bowsprit, 14 Foremast, 15 Main mast, 16 Mizzen mast, 17 Rudder blade, 18 Rudder stock, 19 The steering transmission, 20 Whip-staff, 21 Gallery, 22 Lower deck, 23 embrasure

TABLE II

A cross-section of a modern ship, including its main parts and dimensions (Sea-going, general cargo ship)

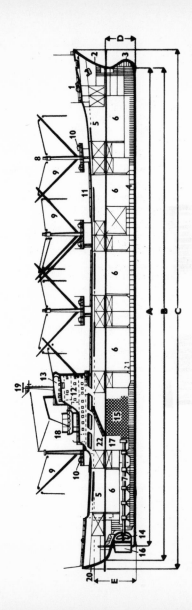

1 Anchor windlass, 2 Stempost, 3 Bulbous bow, 4 Double bottom, 5 Main deck, 6 Cargo holds, 7 Line shafting (stern gear), 8 Masts, 9 Cargo derricks, 10 Cargo winches, 11 Hatchway covers, 12 Superstructure, 13 Navigation bridge, 14 Screw propeller, 15 Main engine, 16 Rudder, 17 Fuel tanks, 18 Davit, 19 Signal mast, 20 Sternpost, 21 Transverse bulkheads, 22 Landing bridge

TABLE III

The main shipbuilding notions and symbols

$L_{o.a.}$ = *Length overall*
The distance between the extreme fore and after, fixed points of the vessel measured in a horizontal projection (this comprises not only the hull but also the parts which are firmly attached to the hull, e.g. the bowsprit, the rudder etc.)

$L_{b.p.}$ = *Length between perpendiculars*
The horizontal distance between the forward and after perpendiculars

$L_{W.L.}$ = *Waterline length*
The length of the main waterline between the forward edge of the stempost and the after edge of the sternpost

$B_{o.a.}$ = *Breadth overall, Beam overall*
The distance between two extreme fixed points in the widest place of the craft measured in a horizontal projection

B_m = *Breadth moulded, Beam moulded*
The maximum horizontal distance between the outside edges of the frames

H = *Depth*
The vertical distance between the upper edge of the deck on the board side of the vessel and the lowest point of the bottom measured on the main waterline

T = *Draught*
The vertical distance between the lowest point of the vessel and water surface

Gross tonnage
The volume of all spaces in the hull and superstructures. It is measured in tons gross (g.t.).

Net tonnage
The volume of the spaces destined for the transportation of cargo. It is measured in tons net (n.t.).

Register ton
The unit of volume used to measure the tonnage of the vessel. It equals 100 cu.ft = 2.83 cubic metres.

Deadweight capacity
The weight of the useful cargo, passengers, luggage, fuel, water and stores, outfit and crew. It is indicated in tons.

Buoyance or total buoyancy
The capacity of a vessel, even when damaged, to float due to the hydrostatic lift in a certain position on the water surface.

Stability
The capacity of the vessel to re-establish the equilibrium position as soon as external forces cease to act.

Displacement
The weight of the water displaced by the vessel. It is indicated in tons.

Main waterline
The plane of intersection of the theoretical shell with the horizontal plane in the height of the moulded draught.

Perpendiculars (persp.)
The vertical lines which go through the points of intersection on the main waterline plane and the fore-edge of the stempost and the after-edge of the sternpost.

SHP = *Shaft horsepower*
The output of the ship's engines, measured in h.p. on the propeller shaft

SM = *Sea mile*
One sixtieth of one equatorial degree (1,852 metres)

kn = *knot*
The speed of a ship, at which 1 sea mile is covered in one hour.

TABLE IV

The classification of water craft

A *According to destination*
1 Civil craft (merchant, trading, recreational and sports craft), 2 Military craft (war and auxiliary vessels), 3 Special (custom, patrol, service and working craft)

B *According to purpose*
1 Passenger ships, 2 Cargo ships and tankers, 3 Mixed ships (passenger/cargo ships), 4 Tugs, 5 Engineering craft, 6 Special vessels, 7 Industrial vessels, 8 Floating equipment

C *According to the area of operation*
1 Sea-going (short-sea, long-distance, coastal, harbour and estuary craft), 2 River and sea-going vessels, 3 Inland (river, lake and canal ships)

D *According to the type of cargo*
1 General cargo (cases, barrels, bales, timber, rolled material, transport vehicles, containers, refrigerated and deep frozen goods), 2 Bulk cargo (coal, grain, ores, fertilisers), 3 Liquid cargo and gases (oil, table oils, wine, molasses, paper pulp etc.)

E *According to ship's propulsion*
1 Self-propelled ships, 2 Non-propelled vessels (rafts, barges and pusher-barges, lighters, pontoons, river ferry prams, floating machines and buildings)

F *According to the power used*
1 Craft propelled by human or animal energy (paddles, oars, poles, with mechanical transmission), 2 Wind-propelled craft (sailing ships, ships propelled by wind wheels or by special wind propulsion, such as the Flettner Rotor Ship), 3 Mechanically propelled craft: a) by steam engines and turbines, b) by internal combustion engines and turbines (with various power gears), c) electrically driven craft (accumulator and trolley), d) ships with special drive (gyroscope ships)

G *According to the system of steam production*
1 Steamers (with steam boilers), 2 Nuclear powered ships (with nuclear reactors)

H *According to the type of ship's propulsion unit*
1 Paddle wheels, oars, paddles, 2 Propellers (screw propeller, Voith-Schneider propeller, aircraft propeller), 3 Water jet propulsion

I *According to the system of navigation*
1 Displacement ships, 2 Skimmers, 3 Hydrofoils, 4 Hovercraft, 5 Undersea craft (submarines, bathyscaphes)

J *According to the hull*
1 Single-hull ships, 2 Single-hull ships with outriggers, 3 Double-hull ships (catamarans), 4 Three-hull and multi-hull ships

K *According to the building material employed*
1 Wood, 2 Steel, 3 Composite, 4 Light alloy, 5 Ferro-concrete, 6 Plastic, 7 Fabric, 8 Made of other natural materials, (leather, reeds, bark etc.)

TABLE V

The classification of ships according to their purpose

1 *Passenger ships*
   a) liners, b) coastal vessels, c) passenger and mail ships, d) cruising or tourist ships, e) pleasure ships and yachts

2 *Cargo ships*
   a) transport of general cargo, b) transport of road and rail vehicles, c) transport of containers, d) transport of timber, e) transport of refrigerated cargo, f) transport of deep frozen foods, g) transport of bulk cargo, h) tankers for carrying liquids, i) tankers for conveying compressed gases, j) others

3 *Mixed ships*
   for the transport of passengers and cargo

4 *Tugs*
   a) tugs, b) push boats, c) pushing tugs

5 *Engineering craft*
   a) floating dredgers and hoppers, b) floating cranes, c) floating pile drivers, d) floating elevators and conveyors e) salvage vessels, f) working vessels (anchor laying and handling pontoons), g) drilling and quarrying ships

6 *Special miscellaneous vessels*
   a) ferryboats (for passengers, for cars and passengers, for trains), b) icebreakers, c) fireboats, d) rescue cruisers, lifeboats and rafts, e) pilot vessels and pilot launches, f) cable-laying ships, g) lightships and tenders, h) hospital ships, i) school or training ships, j) depth survey, hydrographic and research ships, k) display ships, l) other special ships

7 *Industrial vessels*
   a) fishing craft (fishing, transport, auxiliary, processing and whaling ships), b) for fishing and harvesting other sea animals (e.g. lobsters, sponges, oysters), c) exploitation and drilling ships (to gather oil, minerals and ores from the seabed)

8 *Floating equipment*
   a) floating docks, b) floating garages, c) floating depots, d) floating hotels and accommodation ships, e) floating restaurants, f) floating workshops, g) floating gas stations and floating battery recharging stations

TABLE VI

The main categories of recent warships

A *Surface ships*

    I Armed mainly with guns:
        1 Battleships, 2 Heavy cruisers, 3 Light cruisers, 4 Destroyers, 5 General purpose frigates, 6 Escort ships, 7 Fast gunboats, 8 Patrol ships, 9 Gunboats, 10 Vessels for coast defence

    II For the transport of aircraft and helicopters:
        1 Aircraft carriers, 2 Seaplane carriers, 3 Helicopter support ships

    III Armed with missiles:
        1 Missile cruisers, 2 Missile destroyers

    IV Armed with anti-aircraft guns:
        1 Anti-aircraft cruisers
        2 Anti-aircraft frigates

    V Having anti-submarine armaments:
        1 Anti-submarine cruisers, 2 Anti-submarine destroyers, 3 Anti-submarine frigates

    VI Armed mainly with torpedo tubes:
        1 Torpedo-boat destroyers, 2 Torpedo boats, 3 Fast patrol boats, 4 Coastal patrol boats

    VII Mine handling ships:
        1 Minelayers, 2 Minesweepers (inshore), 3 Minesweepers (offshore coastal), 4 Mine hunters

    VIII Landing craft
        1 Troop landing boats, 2 Tank landing boats, 3 Tank landing ships

B *Undersea ships*
    1 Missile submarines, 2 Attack submarines, 3 High-speed, attack submarines, 4 Normal type submarines

C *Auxiliary warships*
    1 Troopers, 2 Supply ships (cargo ships and tenders), 3 Submarine depot ships, 4 Destroyer supply ships, 5 Minesweeper supply ships, 6 Aircraft direction frigates, 7 Research ships, 8 Repair and maintenance ships, 9 Salvage ships (coastal and ocean-going), 10 Diving trial ships, 11 Training sailing ships, 12 Artillery training ships, 13 Special auxiliary ships (cable ships, ice patrol ships, tenders)

TABLE VII

The main types of rigging in sports yachts and small sailing boats

Cutter   Yawl   Ketch

Sloop, older type   Bermudan sloop   Schooner

TABLE VIII

The main types of rigging in great sailing vessels

Brig

Four-masted, full-rigged ship

Three-masted schooner

Schooner brig

Schooner barque

Barque

TABLE IX

The holders of the Blue Ribbon in the twentieth century

Name of the Ship	Country	The year when the Blue Ribbon was gained	Speed attained in knots	Tonnage in tons gross	Principal dimensions $L_{a \cdot o} \times B_m$	Output of the main engines	Number of passengers
Mauretania	Great Britain	1907	26.9	35,674	231.64 × 26.82	70,925	2,165
Bremen	Germany	1929	27.91	51,636	274 × 31	125,000	2,224
Rex	Italy	1933	29.61	51,061	253.1 × 29.5	144,000	1,936
Normandie	France	1935 1937	30.31 31.2	83,243	313.75 × 35.9	160,000	1,975
Queen Mary	Great Britain	1936 1938	30.63 31.69	81,235	310.74 × 35.97	162,176	2,139
United States	U.S.A.	1952	35.59	53,329	301.8 × 30.97	240,000	2,008

TABLE X

A survey of world merchant fleets

Ships (steam and motor) of a tonnage exceeding 100 tons gross according to their nationality (in thousands of tons gross).

Liberia	44,444
Japan	34,929
Great Britain and Northern Ireland	28,625
Norway	23,507
U.S.S.R.	16,734
Greece	15,329
U.S.A.	15,024
Federal Republic of Germany	8,516
Italy	8,187
Panama	7,794
France	7,420
Sweden	5,632
Netherlands	4,972
Spain	4,300
Denmark	4,020
India	2,650
Canada	2,381
Cyprus	2,015
Poland	2,013
Brazil	1,885
Finland	1,630
Yugoslavia	1,588
China (Taiwan)	1,495
Argentina	1,401
German Democratic Republic	1,198
Belgium	1,192
Australia	1,184
People's Republic of China	1,181

World total (thousands tons gross) 268,340

In this total world tonnage oil-tankers occupy 105.129,000 tons and ore and bulk carriers 48.415,000 tons.

The number of the ships of all types with a tonnage exceeding 100,000 tons gross is now 239. This number is made up of 228 oil-tankers and 11 ore/bulk/oil carriers.

More than one half of merchant shipping (62%) is less than 10 years old; 65% of the ships (from total tonnage) are driven by diesel engines. This means that 50,592 vessels are motor ships out of the total number of 57,391.

The statistical data for this table were taken from Lloyd's Register of Shipping, 1972.

EGYPTIAN SEA-GOING VESSEL

The appearance of the ship is illustrated on a relief in the temple Dar-el-Bahar, dating back to the rule of Queen Hatshepsut, that is, roughly 1500 BC. Imported cedar wood was used to build these ships. The ship was up to 98 feet long, and was relatively wide, with a flat bottom, and thus adapted for navigation on the Nile. To support the elevated bow and stern, a powerful hawser was used which bound both ends of the vessel. It was guided through a series of supports amidships and then twisted by a special beam. The ship's structure consisted of beams fitted one on top of the other and held together by dowels. Instead of rope bands, which in older Egyptian ships girded the

upper part of the shell, the transverse structure was strengthened by deck beams protruding the sides of the hull and connected to it by wooden nails. Keel, posts and frames were not then known as structural features. Ships of this time had decks and platforms fore and aft, where the commander of the ship and the helmsmen stood. The stern of the ship was decorated by a lotus flower. The ship was driven by approximately thirty rowers standing on each side, and was also provided with a square sail which could be lowered down. This was extended between two yardarms and attached to a fixed mast. One steering oar with a widened blade was suspended from each side.

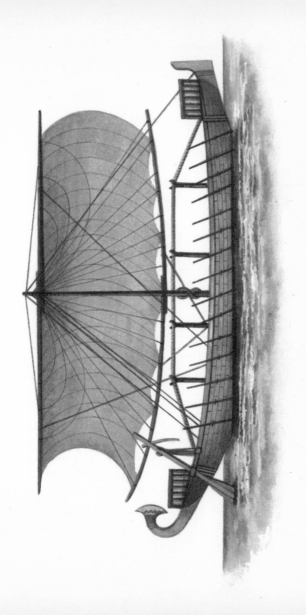

Representations of this ship have been found on remains of the royal palace of Nimrud in old Nineveh, which dates back to about 700 BC. The illustration depicts navigation on the Tigris river. The ship was a warship, probably built by Phoenician architects out of cedar wood. It had a keel prolonged into a bow, in the form of a cone-shaped bow ram. It is debatable whether the ram was used in war or simply resembled the head of a fish or completed the shape of the ship with a lunar crescent. The stempost of the ship was vertical, the stern rounded, the sides

were high and fenced to protect the two banks of rowers. In comparison with Egyptian ships, the deck was reinforced to enable warriors to stand on it, protected from the sides by round shields. As well as oars the ship had one square sail set with upper yard on a fixed mast. Again unlike Egyptian ships, the sail was provided with buntlines, controlled from the deck. The steering of the ship depended on two steering oars, fixed on either side of the stern. The length of the ship was about 98 feet and the draught roughly 6.5 feet.

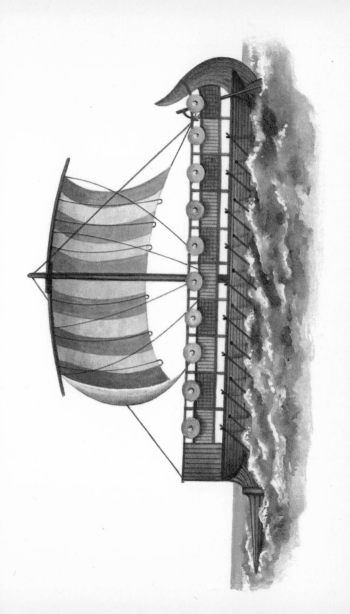

These ships appeared in the second half of the sixth century BC and are partially shown in a frieze found in the temple of Erechtheum on the Athenian Acropolis. The centre line of the hull had an oak backbone to which the ribs were attached. The keel terminated in the bow in a sharp, metal-plated ram, whereas in the stern the backbone ran into a sternpost which was bent forward over the deck and rounded off by a fan or goose's or swan's head. The trireme was steered from a slightly elevated after platform by two steering oars, which had broad blades and were suspended from the sides of the craft. The ship was propelled by three banks of rowers, placed one above the other. The upper bank of oars was mounted on the outriggers, and each oar was

handled by one seated rower. The lower banks of rowers were encased by the hull. The trireme often carried up to 170 oars. Its detachable mast with a square sail was used only in a favourable wind and was lowered before battle. Later triremes had an additional, lower mast in the bow, which inclined forward and had a square sail. The sails were controlled by ropes guided by pulleys. In addition to the bow ram, the main assault force in the triremes were warriors, standing on the upper deck.

The trireme had a length of up to 118 feet, a beam of 20 feet and a draught of 3.2 feet. It was a speedy, easily manoeuvrable ship. The crew, including warriors, numbered approximately two hundred men.

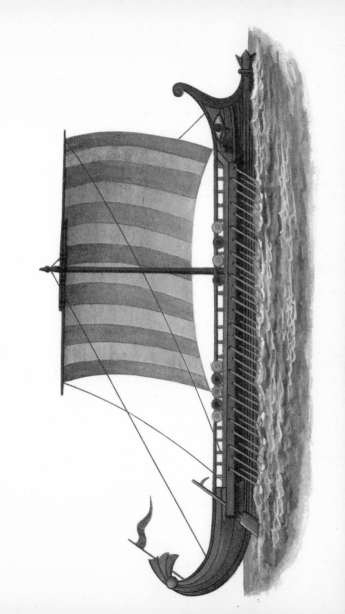

The Roman bireme, dating from the Carthaginian wars for the mastery of the Mediterranean Sea, can be found illustrated in friezes of that period. It was a clumsy ship with a frame structure and a keel which terminated in the bow in a three-hooked ram and raised posts. The sternpost was generally connected to the bulwark, protecting the soldiers on board. The sternpost was shaped like a palm leaf. The bow and the stern of the ship were richly decorated with carvings. The ship was propelled by two banks of rowers, protected by side planking, with several rowers operating each oar. Amidships there was generally a mast with a big square sail that could be taken in, whilst the bow carried an inclined mast which had a smaller square sail. The shelter for the ship's commander was situated aft. The ship was steered by two steering oars suspended from each side of the ship. For engaging the enemy, the ship's bow was provided with a drawbridge, ballast and hooks. The bridge could be rotated in all directions and was suspended on a mast eight metres high. After the enemy ship was hooked, the bridge was used for the assault by Roman armoured warriors. Turret superstructures were built fore and sometimes aft to house various catapults and archers. The Romans' superiority at sea was due to the power and armour of their ships and their ability to adapt infantry techniques to fighting on the decks of enemy ships.

The appearance of these ships can be judged from illustrations on the sarcophagae of Roman ship-owners of the second century BC. Compared with Greek ships, Roman ships had a much fuller shape, a reinforced structure and improved construction on the keel and posts. The sternpost was extended and finished in the form of a swan's or goose's head. The stern carried a superstructure for the commander of the ship and the passengers. A significant improvement was the protection of the underwater part of the ship's hull by thin lead sheathing. The side planking was usually strengthened by outer wales. The ship carried two masts, of which the main one was placed in the middle of the ship and bóre a big, square sail. Sometimes a smaller triangular topsail was suspended over this, and usually cut into two parts because of the forestay. A smaller mast — artemon — ran obliquely above the bow, and from this a smaller square sail was suspended. This mast was used in harbour as a cargo boom. The control and shortening of sails by means of ropes guided over pulleys and purchases was commonplace. Standing rigging consisting of fore and back stays and shrouds with lanyards and deadeyes could be seen here for the first time. Two rudders were suspended on each side of the ship and geared to tillers for steering the ship. Generally the ship had two anchors, weighing 20–25 kg each, and they were stowed on the deck with their rope.

The ship's length varied between 100–150 feet (30–45 metres), the beam 30–40 feet (9–12 metres) and the deadweight capacity 100–150 tons.

The sea-going ships of the Germanic ancestors of contemporary Danes and Norwegians dominated the coastal waters of northern Europe from the fifth to the twelfth centuries AD, helped to conquer and colonise England, discovered Iceland and Greenland and, about AD 1000, landed in North America in what is today known as New Foundland.

Viking ships, also called drakars, were slender, keeled vessels with a solid frame structure and clinker planking, which was held together by wooden pins and pivots. The bow and stern were sharp and similarly shaped (doubleended ships) whilst the fore and sternposts rose high above the ship and generally terminated in the form of a dragon's or spiral head. Oak was the standard building material. The ships reached a length of 80 feet (25 metres), had no decks, only a floor, and were propelled by at least 16 oars on each side. They carried a big square sail that could be lowered and the mast could be dipped and pulled up. A broad oar with an attached tiller served as a side rudder. Generally it was pivoted on the starboard side. The rowers were protected against bad weather and danger by circular shields, hung at the sides; occasionally a tent shelter was erected in the stern.

Many of the Viking ships which have been excavated, have been deposited in naval museums in the Scandinavian countries, as for example those in Nydam, Oseberg, Gokstad and Kvalsund. A striking visual account of how the Normans, who crossed the Channel to conquer England in 1066, built their ships, and the shape of them, is shown on the Bayeux Tapestry, which dates from the second half of the eleventh century.

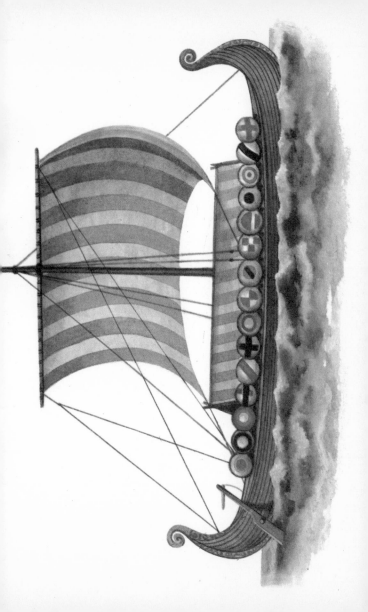

Ships of this type dominated the Mediterranean in the twelfth and thirteenth centuries, during the Crusades and pilgrimages to the Holy Land. They began as rounded merchantmen, often adapted to carry a great many people, animals and bulk cargo. Such ships had a rib construction, complete decks, and a rounded bow and stern, the sides of which were overhung by superstructures called castles. Originally these castles were platforms with rails and only later did they merge into the hull of the ship. The rails of such castles were decorated with the emblems of nobility. For protection against the weather, the castles were covered by a tent roof. The ship was propelled by sails. Initially it had one high mast and a lateen sail set amidships; later another mast appeared at the bow which was also set with a lateen sail. Both masts were placed relatively close to each other. On the tops of these masts were sometimes crow's nests, which were used not only as look-outs but also for fighting. The ship was steered by two steering oars, suspended from the sides of the vessel in the stern.

Various commercial contracts of this period and descriptions left by crusaders, provide us with a picture of these ships and the difficult life at sea. The crew numbered about 130, and the ship had a waterline length of up to 103 feet, a beam of 47 feet, a deadweight capacity of 560 tons and carried several hundred passengers.

The major type of medieval merchantman in Northern and Baltic waters was the cog, which developed from ships used by the inhabitants of the Frisian Islands and from the hulks and huge river craft of the lower Rhine and Meuse. Its name derived from the wine barrels, initially the main cargo of such cogs on the journeys between England and the European continent. Cogs were clinker-built, keeled ships and had a complete deck, a spoon bow and a rounded stern to which the rudder was centrally attached. This stern rudder, together with a great square sail, set on a high mast amidships, were the typical features of the cog. Fore and aft, there were solid superstructures — the castles — which overhung the main contour of the ship. They were used to provide accommodation and for fighting. In the fifteenth century another smaller foremast was added to the main mast; this had a square sail and later a third, even smaller, mast was located aft and set with a lateen sail. The bowsprit, mounted alongside the stempost, served not only to lower the anchor and to load goods but also to fix the stays of the foremast. Crow's nests were placed on the top of the main and foremasts.

Cogs became the most commonly used craft of the Union of European Harbour Towns, the Hansa, which was founded in 1241 and they served both as transport and military vessels in the constant battle against pirates and such competing countries as England and Denmark. In the thirteenth century their average deadweight capacity was 200 tons, but by the end of the fifteenth century it had increased to 570 tons.

This type of ship began life in the Mediterranean as an imitation of the northern cog. Compared with the cog, the carrack had a greater size, fuller shape, higher sides and a greater surface area along the main waterline than along its upper deck. Fore and aft, they usually had two-deck superstructures, or castles, which narrowed towards the centre. The forecastle extended into the overhanging triangular bow, called the carrack bow, whilst the aftercastle was rectangular and usually not higher than the forecastle. Instead of one mast, as in the cog, the carrack had two additional masts, the mizzen mast with a lateen sail and a short mast in the forecastle, set with a small square sail. An inclined mast, the forerunner of the later bowsprit, protruded from the bow and was used for securing the stays of the foremast and later carried a small square sail. The hull planking was strengthened externally, near the mainmast shrouds, by massive outer wales. Steering was by a stern rudder, as in cogs. As soon as carracks appeared in the Atlantic and the North Sea, the sailors of these regions adopted them and quickly improved upon them. The main and foremasts were extended and the great square sails were completed by one small square topsail each, which improved the manoeuvrability of such craft. Columbus' flagship, the *Santa Maria*, was a smaller type of carrack. The topsail was fitted on the main mast and a lower castle was located in the bow. Her dimensions were: length 75 feet, beam 22 feet, draught 9 feet and displacement 237 tons. She carried a crew of ninety men.

CARAVEL

Caravels were born in the Mediterranean. The shape of their hull and their triangular sails were reminiscent of Arabic craft of the same region. Originally they were small ships whose weight did not exceed 200 tons and had a single, forward inclined mast and a big lateen sail. They were fast ships and easily manoeuvrable. Later caravels were finely shaped and had two or three masts and lateen sails. Sometimes the foremast had a square sail instead of a lateen one. An extended castle was erected in the stern of the ship. Caravels had a relatively small draught and later reached a deadweight of 400 tons. The hull was smooth and made of carvel-built planks. The ship was steered by a stern rudder.

The *Pinta* and the *Nina*, the other ships of Columbus'

fleet, were caravels. Opinions as to their shape and rigging differ, although it is known that in the Canary Islands Columbus substituted the lateen sail of the *Pinta* for a square one.

Dimensions:	*Pinta*	*Nina*
Length	65.9 feet (20.1 m)	56.7 feet (17.3 m)
Beam	23.9 feet (7.3 m)	18.3 feet (5.6 m)
Draught	6.5 feet (2.0 m)	6.2 feet (1.9 m)
Displacement	167.4 tons	101.2 tons
Crew	65	40

This four-masted carrack was built by Henry VIII (1509–1547) and modelled on carracks built in Genoa and Lübeck. She was Henry's flagship. The ship was launched in 1514 and with a deadweight of 1,000 tons, she constituted the greatest ship of her time. The 'Great Harry', as the ship was affectionately called, was 167 feet long, had 8 decks, 180 guns and a huge surface area of sail. In 1520 Henry VIII, leading his navy, sailed on her from Dover bound for France, along with 700 crew and soldiers and 385 guns of various sizes. However, because of her instability, she could not make the open sea in the face of strong winds. As a result, she was completely rebuilt between 1536 and 1539 and ultimately had 6 decks, 151 heavy guns and a protective shield to fend off grappling irons. The hull was strengthened and had carvel planking, and the rigging was considerably improved in comparison with other carracks of the period. Altogether this ship had twelve sails, including a square sail on the bowsprit, three square sails on the fore and mainmasts and three and two lateen sails on the mizzen mast and on the bonaventure (fourth mast). Only the high superstructures bore any relation to the previous system of construction.

The 'Great Harry' never took part in a naval engagement but nevertheless her rigging and structural modifications represent a further stage in the development of ship design. In 1553 she was destroyed by fire.

The galleon was the ship type developed from the carrack in the sixteenth century by Spanish and Portuguese sailors and shipwrights and adapted for the commercial and military needs of this colonising age. Galleons were bigger than carracks, more stream-lined in shape, with a length of around 164 feet, a beam of 46 feet, and a displacement of 1,600 tons. The number of masts, originally four, finally settled at three. The masts were assembled and set with three or four square sails. The mizzen mast usually had a lateen sail, whilst the bowsprit, connected to an extended stempost, called the beak-head, carried a square sail. Galleons also had more-deck castles, which were higher aft than fore, although the height of such castles was not so great as those of the carracks and generally the slope of the upper deck became levelled. The aftercastle had galleries which were richly decorated by carvings. The stern of the ship

was a flat, transom type. Such galleons formed the basis of the Spanish naval and merchant marine, and because of their good navigational features were adopted by other maritime nations, among which the English later became famous as galleon builders. They perfected the armaments of this vessel and made further improvements, which resulted in the creation of a standard type of full-rigged man-of-war.

An example of this sophisticated craft was the *Sovereign of the Seas*. Built in England by Phineas Pett in 1637, she was the biggest and most beautiful warship of the time. For the first time science, in the form of applied mathematics and geometry, was used in her construction. Her armament consisted of 100 guns, located on all three decks. Displacing 1,700 tons, she had a hull 172.5 feet (56.5 metres) long, an overall length of 232 feet (76 metres), and a beam of 46.5 feet (15.2 metres).

Medieval rowing galleys developed from their ancient Greek and Roman counterparts and from their descendents, the Dalmatian liburns and Byzantine dromons. From the eleventh century onwards they were one of the main types of craft of the Italian City States and were used both for commercial and military purposes. In the sixteenth century they had a length of 150 feet (45 metres), a beam of 23 feet (7.5 metres) and were propelled by 48 oars, each 40 feet long (13 metres). Each oar was handled by three rowers. In the eighteenth century their maximum dimensions were: length 170 feet (56 metres), beam 26 feet (8.5 metres) and they had 51 oars with five men on each and a displacement of 200 to 280 tons. Such galleys generally had two or three masts, each with big lateen sails, which were suspended from dual sectioned yardarms. War galleys had a forecastle or battery, which was usually equipped with five guns. The stern bore a further superstruc-

ture which overhung both sides of the vessel and provided quarters for the captain and the officers in command of the soldiers on board, who were used to attack enemy ships after they had been hooked.

Characteristic features of galleys were their sharp, protruding rams and their rich decorations, which took the form of carvings, flags and laces. At first free citizens were hired as oarsmen but later prisoners of war, slaves and criminals were used almost exclusively and their living conditions on board were often inhuman. In the Battle of Lepanto in 1571, often called the battle of the galleys, more than 100 vessels took part in the action on both sides. Galleys remained an important type of vessel in the French navy of Louis XIV as late as the end of the seventeenth century.

After galleys, oars were only used sporadically as a means of propulsion in coastal navigation and in certain types of small vessels.

In 1620 the three-masted *Mayflower*, with a party of 130 English Puritans on board, left Plymouth under the command of Captain Jones of Rotherhithe and reached the coast of North America near present-day Massachusetts after a voyage lasting 67 days. Here the Puritans founded the first permanent English settlement in New England. According to existing records, the *Mayflower* was originally built about 1590 to carry wine and had a deadweight capacity of 180 tons. On the basis of a model made in 1926 by Dr R.C. Anderson and at present located in the Pilgrim's Hall, Plymouth, Massachusetts, a replica of the original ship was built in 1956. This Mayflower had carrack rigging and generally the appearance of a small galleon. On 17 April 1957 the *Mayflower II* set sail with a crew of 33 under the command of Captain Alan Villiers from the small fishing port of Brixham in Devon. She left Plymouth on 20 April and reached Plymouth, Massachusetts, after 54 days. While the *Mayflower* of the Pilgrim Fathers took a direct route across the Atlantic, *Mayflower II* took a southern route by way of Madeira and the Canary Islands. She covered the distance of 5,500 sea miles in thirteen days less than her famous mother-ship in 1620.

This type of ship provided the basis for Dutch commercial power in the seventeenth century. The construction of Dutch fluyts began in 1595 in the Dutch town of Hoorn and in the course of only twenty years the type was fully developed. The main feature of Dutch fluyts was a closer relationship between length and beam that had hitherto been usual ($4\frac{1}{2}$:1). The full form along the waterline together with the quickly narrowing sides of the ship gave it a pouchy appearance. The deck was steeply inclined and narrowed towards the stern, terminating in an unostentatious superstructure that had developed from the sterncastle. In comparison with galleons, Dutch fluyts had above a rounding stern a high narrow transom. The flat, narrowing rear wall of the super-

structure protruded above the stern. The tiller of the stern rudder was controlled from an oval opening in the stern. This aperture was also used for loading longer items of cargo, such as timber. The Dutch fluyts had three relatively high masts, of which the fore and the mainmasts had two square sails each, whilst the mizzen mast carried a lateen sail. A sprit sail was set on the bowsprit. Dutch fluyts were up to 120–140 feet long and 22–26.5 feet wide, and were equipped with four to six guns for their protection.

Because of the simplified rigging, Dutch fluyts did not need a large crew and the use of these ships very quickly spread throughout western Europe. They were also employed in the West Indies trade.

In 1638, one year after the English launched their powerful galleon, the *Sovereign of the Seas*, equipped with 100 guns, the *Couronne* was launched in Roche-Bernard in France. The *Couronne* was the first ship built according to the scientific specifications contained in the theoretical work 'L'Hydrographie', by Father Fournier. The *Couronne* was a three-masted galleon with two gun decks, displacing 2,181 tons. The distinctive feature of the ship was a long beak-head deck with a low protruding stempost, which allowed forward fire and protected the ship against galleys. The fore and mainmasts were set with three square sails, the mizzen mast was set with a lateen sail and a square topsail. Another square sail was set on the bowsprit. The surface area of the sails amounted to about 12,000 square metres.

The *Couronne* had a bow richly decorated by painted carvings, and similar ornamentation could be found on the stern superstructure, which was fitted with galleries and high arcaded windows. Compared with the *Sovereign of the Seas*, the *Couronne* had only 80 guns, although in effect the same fire power, since the lower row of guns on board the English galleon could not be used at sea because of her inferior stability.

The *Couronne* proved herself an excellent ship, and served as a model for the construction of many other ships.

Dimensions: length of the hull on the main waterline 166.3 feet (50.7 metres), maximum beam 49 feet (14.9 metres), depth (to the main deck) 17.9 feet (6 metres).

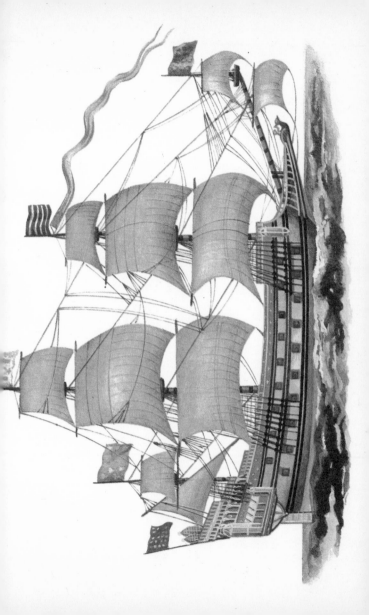

In the seventeenth century, European countries were beginning to extend their trade to the Far East, India and Sunda Islands. For mutual strength and organisation in this trade, ship owners and tradesmen formed special companies. In 1600 the East India Company was formed in England. Very soon the ships of these societies dominated the whole maritime trade of the Far East; initially the Dutch were the most prominent, later the English and finally the French.

Craft adapted to the conditions of these voyages, which could take up to one year, developed from the galleon and the Dutch fluyt. East Indiamen were three-masted, generally full-rigged ships with two decks and three square sails on each mast, a long bowsprit and two jibs. The superstructure was erected only aft and extended to the main mast. Since the ships sailed in zones infested by pirates, East India-men were heavily armed and had one row of guns on the upper deck. The hull was full and adapted to carry as much cargo as possible. Because of the duration of the voyages and innumerable difficulties, these ships had a large crew. By the beginning of the seventeenth century the greatest sailing ships of the East India Company had attained a deadweight of 700 tons. In the course of the eighteenth century their average capacity had risen to 1,200 tons, and by the middle of the nineteenth century it was 1,500 tons and they were built as three-deckers. Because of their great size and armaments, they were more like the smaller contemporary warships. The age of the East Indiamen ended in the fifties of the nineteenth century, when maritime trade began to need faster transport, and their task was taken over by the clippers.

The *Victory* was Admiral Lord Nelson's flagship, on board which he died, off Trafalgar in October 1805. This battle, in which the British navy under the command of Admirals Nelson and Collingwood, defeated the allied Franco-Spanish navy under Admiral Villeneuve, decided the destiny of Napoleonic Europe. From then, up to the Second World War, Great Britain retained the position of the greatest sea power in the world.

The *Victory* was a five-deck, three-masted, first rate ship of the line with three gun decks, 102 guns and a crew of 850 men. The ship was designed by Sir Thomas Slade, controller of the British navy. Her keel was laid in 1759 in Chatham dockyard and the ship was launched in May 1765. The original armament consisted of 104 guns, of which 30 were long 32-pounders. In 1793 the number of guns was increased to 110. From 1790 *Victory* was the flagship of Lord Hood and proved herself in actions against the Spaniards and French. In 1797 she took part in the battle against the Spanish fleet off St Vincent. In the years 1801—1803, she was once more rebuilt. At the end of April 1803, she became the flagship of Lord Nelson who was given the command of the Mediterranean fleet. In 1806 she was repaired and served until 1815 when she was placed in reserve in Portsmouth. Today she flies the flag of the Commander-in-Chief, and is one of the few preserved wooden warships in Britain.

Dimensions: length o.a. 226.5 feet (69 metres), maximum beam 52 feet (15.9 metres), depth of hold 21.5 feet (6.6 metres), displacement 2,162 tons.

In 1787 George III (1760–1820) instructed Lt. William Bligh to obtain breadfruit seeds in Tahiti and take them to the West Indies for cultivation. Bligh set sail on 24 December 1787 in the direction of Cape Horn in a three-masted, full-rigged ship called the *Bounty* with a crew of 44 men. Because of stormy weather he could make little progress westwards and therefore turned to the east and went round the Cape of Good Hope. After eleven months he reached Tahiti where he had been eleven years before as Captain Cook's helmsman. After half a year's trading and after taking on board breadfruit seed, the *Bounty* set out on the return journey. On 28 April 1789 in the neighbourhood of the islands of Tofua the majority of the crew revolted under the leadership of the second mate, Fletcher Christian, and set Captain Bligh and eighteen companions adrift in a small open boat with a minimum of food. After a difficult voyage Bligh and his companions reached the island of Timor at the end of 42 days, having covered 3,701 miles. This voyage without loss of life is considered one of the most remarkable journeys ever made as Bligh had only a compass to help him.

The *Bounty* returned to Tahiti where sixteen of the mutineers had stayed. Fletcher and the remaining eight members of the crew and nineteen natives retired to the island of Pitcairn, which lies 1300 miles southeast of Tahiti. The *Topaz* from Boston rediscovered these remaining mutineers eighteen years later.

The *Bounty* was a rebuilt merchantman with a deadweight of 217 tons, an overall length of 91 feet (27.73 metres), a beam of 24.3 feet (7.42 metres), and a depth of 19 feet (5.8 metres). She was equipped with four large and ten small cannon.

No authentic illustration of the *Bounty* has been preserved. The plate opposite was made from the replica for the second film version of 1960.

The frigate was one of the smaller warships of the eighteenth century and proved herself to be an excellent patrol and escort vessel. She was a sailing ship of the 5th line and was equipped with one gun deck and more than 32 guns. Frigates as a type of ship originated in France about the middle of the eighteenth century and had two decks and a length of between 120 and 128 feet (36.5 to 38 metres). They were fast, adaptable ships and by the beginning of the nineteenth century, had proved their worth during the American colonies' struggle for independence.

The frigate *Constitution*, popularly called '*Old Iron-sides*', was a two-deck, three-masted wooden ship and was full-rigged. Her keel was laid in 1795 at Hartt's shipyard in Boston under the design of Joshua Humphrey from Philadelphia. She was launched in October 1797 and ended her trials in 1798. Her hull was copper-plated and her armament consisted of 44 guns, of which 30 were long 24-pounders.

Immediately after completion, the *Constitution* entered the service of the U.S. Navy, along with the frigates *Constellation* and *United States*, with the object of protecting merchant shipping. All three gained experience in the war against France from 1801 to 1805 and as a result were prepared to meet the British blockade of the American coastline in 1812. The *Constitution*, under the command of Captain Isaac Hull, succeeded in running the blockade of the British ships and later defeated the frigates *Guerrière* and *Java* and other enemy ships in the years 1812 to 1814. In the thirties of this century the *Constitution* was restored and anchored as the only remaining eighteenth-century frigate in the U.S. Naval Shipyard in Boston.

Dimensions: length of the gun deck 175 feet (53.5 metres), beam 43.5 feet (13.3 metres), depth of hold 14.3 feet (4.36 metres), displacement 1,576 tons.

By the beginning of the nineteenth century the development of trade called for a speedier carriage of goods and hence faster sea-going ships. American shipbuilders in New York and Boston, drawing on the experience obtained in designing the hulls of schooners, vessels which had attained high speeds, removed everything that served no useful function from the waterline upwards. They made the shape of their ships more slender by increasing the ratio of length to beam until it was between 5 and 6 to 1; in the process they created the clipper, a type of fast sailing ship. The clipper had very tall masts which were made up of four sections. The foremast was moved closer to the ship's centre and the bowsprit reduced in length. The usual sail arrangement, consisting of square sails, was retained, but the number of sails was increased to seven on any one mast, and the number of stay sails set between the masts was reduced. This design did much to simplify manoeuvres. Initially the clipper was three-masted but later, particularly when steel began to be used in the construction of the hull, there were four and even five masts.

At the end of the first half of the nineteenth century the American clippers began to plough the oceans of the world and before long their speed had given them virtual monopolies of certain cargoes, especially the transport of tea from Asia to England. Clipper races with cargoes on board were soon organised and followed with enormous interest. The most famous clippers involved were the *Flying Cloud*, *Rainbow*, *Sovereign of the Seas* and *Westward Ho*.

In the 1860s England began to build clippers and soon English clippers built in London docks were competing with the Americans. The most famous race took place in 1866 when the clippers *Ariel* and *Teaping* reached London almost simultaneously, after voyages from China which had taken 99 and 101 days respectively.

One of the best known clippers of the second half of the nineteenth century was the three-masted *Cutty Sark*, built in Scotland, which, after being withdrawn from active service, was installed in dry dock at Greenwich as a lasting reminder of the glorious era of the sailing ships.

This type of sailing ship was developed in the United States of America at the beginning of the eighteenth century and was designed for use on the open sea. The slender shape of the ship's hull, with its relatively small freeboard and nearly plane deck were adapted from the French frigates that came to the American continent during the War of Independence. Another feature of the schooner was its sharply pointed bow, intended to cut through the waves, as opposed to the bows of older types of craft that met the water with a wide surface area. The schooner differed from earlier sailing ships in her rigging; she had both fore-and-aft sails or gaff sails and focs as they were called. Typical schooners were two-masted, then later three-masted and ultimately multi-masted. The first four-masted schooner was the *William L. White*, built in 1880; the first five-masted schooner was the *Governor Ames* of 1888 and the first six-masted one, with fore-and-aft sails, was the *George W. Wells*, built

in 1900. The only schooner ever to have seven masts, the *Thomas W. Lawson*, was built in 1902.

Later square topsails were added to the fore-and-aft sails. By various permutations of these sails and the square sails, other categories of sailing ships of the schooner type arose, such as the schooner barque, the schooner brig, etc. Their common feature was tremendous speed, sometimes as much as 20 knots. They also had a relatively shallow draught and easily manageable rigging, which required only a small crew.

The medium-sized schooner reached a length of some 98 feet. The first schooners were built in Baltimore and their speed became commonplace along both coasts of the U.S.A. and later in other areas. On the west coast they were used for carrying timber, and on the east coast mainly for coal. Later schooners were built for fishing, commercial and sporting purposes.

In the 1880s, after the opening of the Suez Canal, the competition between sailing ships and steam-driven ones intensified. Shipbuilders started to construct huge multi-masted, full-rigged ships with iron or steel hulls of 4,000 to 5,000 tons. Such ships reached a length of 425 feet (130 metres) and a beam of 55 feet (16.5 metres) which meant that the ratio of the length to the breadth was increased to almost 8:1. The ships were destined to carry bulk cargoes and on their voyages reached formidable speeds in excess of 20 knots. The Germans in particular became famous for building the four- and five-masted sailing ships. Their ships of this type were still in use in the middle of this century. The best known were the sailing ships of the Flying P-Line, to which belonged the *Preussen* (the largest of all with a displacement of 11,400 tons), the *Padua*, *Pasat*, *Potosi*, and *Pamir* (which sank in a storm in September 1957).

The five-masted sailing ship *Kjøbenhavn* was built between 1914 and 1921 in the naval yards of Ramage and Ferguson in Leith, Scotland, for the Danish East Asian Company of Copenhagen and was one of the greatest sailing ships built at the beginning of the twentieth century. The model used for her design was the five-masted *Potosi*, built in 1895, which reached a record speed of 22.4 knots in 1900. The ship had an all-iron hull, a long poop and behind the mizzen mast was a small superstructure, containing the wheel house. Four masts carried twenty-four square sails, whilst the jigger mast was equipped with a double gaff sail. The total surface area of the sails was 56,000 square feet (5,200 square metres).

The *Kjøbenhavn* served as a training ship for the Danish merchant fleet and disappeared without a trace near Cape Horn with all her crew during a voyage from Montevideo to Australia in December 1928.

Dimensions: length 390 feet (119 metres), beam 49 feet (14.95 metres), gross tonnage 3,965 tons, output of the auxiliary engine 500 h.p.

THE TRAINING SHIP *DAR POMORZA*

Dar Pomorza is a three-masted full-rigged ship with a sail surface area of 1,926 square metres. She has an auxiliary engine which generates some 470 h.p. Her principal dimensions are: length of hull 233 feet (71 metres), overall length inclusive of bowsprit (91 metres), beam 41 feet (12.5 metres), height of masts 134.5 feet (41 metres). The crew numbers 184 persons.

As a training ship, she is used for naval and merchant sea cadets. At present such sail training ships are owned by only a few countries. The most modern ones are the three-masted British schooners, the *Sir Winston Churchill* and the *Sir Malcolm Miller*. Full-rigged ships include the Danish *Denmark*, the Italian *Amerigo Vespucci*, the Soviet *Towarysch*, the Norwegian *Christian Radich* and *Sørlandet*. The American ships, the 'Eagle' series, the German *Gorch Fock*, the Portuguese *Sagres* and finally the Norwegian *Statsraad Lemkuhl* are rigged like barques whilst the Belgian *Mercator* has barquentine rigging.

The Polish training ship *Dar Pomorza* (the 'Gift of Pomerania') is one of the last of the great full-rigged ships. She is owned by the Polish merchant navy. The *Dar Pomorza* was built in 1909 in the famous Hamburg shipyard Blohm-Voss and named *Prinz Eitel Friedrich*. In the course of the First World War she was anchored in Kiel and served as an accommodation vessel of the German navy. In 1919 as a part of reparations she was handed over to the French government. Her new owner, the Baron de Forest, gave her a new name, the *Colbert*, and intended to remodel her as a luxury yacht but because of high running costs the ship was sold to Poland in 1929. Poland bought her with contributions from the inhabitants of Pomerania. The ship was reconstructed in the Nakskov naval yards in Denmark and in 1930 was incorporated in the Polish navy. During the Second World War the ship was interned in Sweden. In 1934 and 1935 she had made a voyage round the world and many other long-distance journeys, and much later in 1968 she sailed round Europe to the Black Sea.

SAILING CRUISER YACHT

The word yacht (jagt) is of Dutch or Friesian origin and means to run fast or to hurry. Yachts were in fact speedy craft, originally used for pleasure and fishing on river canals and in coastal waters, although later they were employed as patrol and communications vessels. The love of yachts spread from Holland to England, from where, during the ensuing development of yachting, it was re-exported to the continent.

Today, yachts are mainly used for sporting activities. For participation in races they are grouped according to certain criteria, such as type and size of the yacht, and weight of hull, rigging etc. into corresponding racing categories. The sailing cruiser yachts are generally one- or two-masted. When they have two masts, schooner rigging or more often ketch and yawl rigging are used. All these types have fore-and-aft rigging with one or two focs on their bows.

Yachts with only one mast and those with a fore-

mast or bowsprit are called cutters and sloops. Cutter rigging, which includes a main sail and two focs, was employed until the Second World War in all the great racing yachts. Originally the yacht had fore-and-aft sails of a trapezoidal shape with a gaff beam and a gaff yard and they usually carried triangular topsails. In the course of time the triangular fore-and-aft sails became a fixture (bermuda rig), whilst the masts were straight and of one piece. Now, instead of the normal foc sail, balloon-shaped spinnakers are used, because of their traction capacity when the wind is blowing from behind. The bowsprit does not exist in modern cruising yachts and the bow, foc sails are attached to the deck. Cruising yachts usually have a sunken cabin, a cockpit, and a massive keel with ballast. They are generally equipped with an auxiliary, inboard engine. They range from 25 to 50 feet (8 to 15 metres) in length and have accommodation for a crew of between four and six.

JUNK

Junks are counted as primitive vessels because during a thousand years or more they have not changed their appearance. Their design and rigging is nevertheless still very efficient in such navigationally difficult waters as the coasts of the China Sea and its many islands in the monsoon region of East Asia. Junks had stern rudders as early as the fourth century BC and they also had fore-and-aft rigging. For centuries they have had bulkheads dividing up their hulls into watertight compartments. The junk generally has its sails of balance lug type, extended and stiffened by battens, set on two or three masts. The sails can be stretched as in modern yachts and consequently the ship can be controlled quickly and efficiently. The hull of the junk is flat and wide and both ends rise sharply. Junks quickly spread throughout Asia. They are used as fishing, merchant, war, river and sea-going vessels. Junks from northern areas have a bold, spoon bow, transom stern, and more rectangular sails, while junks from the south have arch-shaped sails.

Currently junks reach a length of up to 180 feet (60 metres), have a beam of 28 feet (9 metres) and a deadweight of up to 500 tons.

SAMPAN

This is a small river craft with a wedge-shaped hull and a flat bottom and is generally steered by a stern oar. They are usually driven by oars. A shelter is usually erected on the deck and covered with a curved roof. They have an average length of 28 feet (9 metres). Sampans are used on rivers and in the harbours of the China Sea as houseboats.

PIROGUE

The inhabitants of the coastal regions of Africa, America and Asia and of the Polynesian islands use dug-out canoes, made from tree-trunks for sailing and fishing. They are called dug-outs and are propelled by paddles. As such vessels are not particularly stable, especially in surf, the natives have improved them by using an outrigger, that is, a float placed alongside the boat's hull on one or both sides and attached to an outrigged beam. On one hand vessels thus adapted can carry a larger cargo and on the other they can be set with various types of sail. Sometimes the outrigger assumes the size and shape of another boat, at which point such craft are called catamarans and if they have three hulls, trimarans. Their good sailing features are incorporated into the design of modern sailing and motor boats.

DHOW

The dhow is a typical sailing vessel of the Indian Ocean and is used by Arabs, Persians and Indians. Its smooth, arch-shaped hull is reminiscent of other ancient primitive boats of this region. The sternpost rises obliquely from the water, while the sternpost is nearly perpendicular, sometimes taking the shape of a transom and to which the stern-rudder is attached and controlled by the tiller. The deck is either covered or open, according to the size of the ship and has a shelter or superstructure at the stern. One or two masts carry great Arabic lateen sails, which are not triangular but trapezoidal in shape with a shortened fore edge. These sails are difficult to handle, especially on the long yardarm. They are, however, very satisfactory in moderate monsoon conditions.

Dhows have a length of 70 to 100 feet (25 to 35 metres) and weigh up to 200 tons. They are known under several different names, such as bumboats, zaruqs, sanbuqs etc., according to the locality.

This was the first steamboat to be economically employed on the regular route between New York and Albany on the Hudson River. In the next ployed on the American continent in the waterways season the ship was once again reinforced and rebuilt around New York. The correct name of the ship was and remained in operation until 1814. Using the the *North River* (*Steamboat of Clermont*). She was built design of the *North River*, Fulton built two more ships by Robert Fulton and Robert R. Livingstone in the for the Hudson River in 1810, and in 1811 constructed naval yards of Corlears Hook on the Hudson. She was ed the *New Orleans* which was the first steamboat on long, narrow, flat-bottomed, with a small sheer, and the Mississippi. was made of wood. She was equipped with an English The dimensions of the initial design of *Clermont* steam engine made by Boulton, Watt and Co., were: length o.a. 142 feet (43.28 metres) beam developing some 20 h.p. Fitted with a crank shaft 14 feet (4.28 metres), depth 4 feet (1.22 metres), dis- and transmission gear designed by Fulton, this engine placement 79 tons. drove two side paddle wheels 15 feet in diameter, The dimensions of the second design were: length each wheel bearing eight radial paddles. After the trial o.a. 149 feet (45.41 metres), beam 17.92 feet (5.46 voyage which took place on 17 August 1807, the metres), depth 7 feet (2.13 metres), displacement *North River* was reinforced, cabins were added, and 182 tons. rails provided, and on 4 September 1807 she was

This was the first steam-driven ship to cross the Atlantic in the service of the newly created American firm, the Savannah Steam Ship Co. Later she was rebuilt for passenger transport capable of carrying thirty-two persons. She was built by the naval architect, Francis Fickett, in the Corlears Hook yards in New York. Originally she was designed for packet service for the Le Havre region. She was built of wood and was full-rigged. The 90 h.p. steam engine was only auxiliary and made it possible for her to steam at a speed of 4 knots. The side wheels, with a diameter of 15.25 feet (4.65 metres), had ten paddles which were collapsible when the ship was under sail. The ship left Savannah on 24 May 1819 and arrived in Liverpool on 20 June 1819. During this voyage she used steam for only 85 hours. After unsuccessful attempts by the owners to sell the ship to the U.S. government, the *Savannah* was sold in an auction in 1820; the engine and the paddle wheels were removed and the ship was put into service as a coastal sail-packet ship between Savannah and New York. She was wrecked in November 1821 in a storm near the Long Island coast.

Dimensions: length o.a. 110 feet (33.6 metres), length between perps. 98.5 feet (30.02 metres), beam 25.8 feet (7.86 metres), width over the paddle wheels 36 feet (10.97 metres), draught 13 feet (3.95 metres), gross tonnage 320 tons.

The *Curaçao* was the first steam-driven ship to cross the Atlantic from Europe to South America. She was a three-masted, side-wheeled, wooden steamer, with schooner rigging, built by Messrs. J. H. and J. Duke in Dover. She was launched in September 1825 under the name *Calpe*, and was intended for trade between Great Britain, America and the West Indies. Her owners, the American and Colonial Steam Navigation Co. of London sold her in October 1826 to the Dutch as an addition to the Netherlands Navy, in which she was the first steamer, and was given the name *Curaçao*. In April 1827 the *Curaçao* left Hellevoetsluis near Rotterdam with 57 persons on board bound for Paramaribo, where she arrived on 24 May. The voyage of 4,000 sea miles took 28 days and steam was only partly used. During the voyage technical problems affecting the steam engine and the paddle wheel meant that the paddles had to be changed in midvoyage. The *Curaçao* repeated her voyage across the Atlantic on two more occasions. Between 1830 and 1834 she was used on the river Scheld and in 1840 she was put into service in the West Indies again. In 1846 she was retired from active service and in 1850 sold for scrap.

Dimensions: length between perps. 127·3 feet (38.8 metres), breadth of hull 26.9 feet (8.2 metres), breadth over the paddle boxes 44·9 feet (13·7 metres), depth of hold 16.5 feet (5.03 metres), draught 13.5 feet (4.12 metres), gross tonnage 438 tons. The nominal output of the side-lever steam engines was 100 h.p. She was armed with seven pounders and had a crew of 42.

The first ship to cross the Atlantic under continuous steam power was the *Sirius*. This was a wooden, two-masted side wheeler. Her foremast was set with three square sails and the mainmast was fore-and-aft rigged. The *Sirius* was built in 1837 by Robert Menzies and Son in Leith for the St George Steam Packet Co. and intended to operate between London and Cork. She was the first ship to have surface condensors, capable of feeding the boilers with fresh water. However, as their own ship, the *British Queen*, was not finished in time, the British and American Steam Navigation Company hired the *Sirius* to sail to New York in April 1838. On 4 April 1838 the *Sirius* left Cork harbour with 40 passengers on board bound for New York. After 18 days and 10 hours the ship safely reached her destination despite strong winds. Her average speed was 6.7 knots. The steamer *Great Western* arrived four hours later. In July of the same year the *Sirius* crossed the Atlantic once more. After her return she was put into service between Glasgow and Cork. In January 1847 during one of these voyages, she was wrecked on the rocks in Ballycotton Bay.

Dimensions: length o a. 208 feet (63.4 metres), length between perps. 178.4 feet (54.4 metres), width of the hull 25.8 feet (7.87 metres), width over paddle boxes 47.25 feet (14.4 metres), dep-h of hold 18.3 feet (5.57 metres), draught 15 feet (4.58 metres), tonnage 703 tons. The nominal output of the side-lever steam engines was 320 h.p. The crew numbered 35.

In 1830 an English farmer, F. P. Smith, succeeded in propelling a small boat by means of a wooden screw propeller driven by a 6 h.p. steam engine, and he was commissioned by the British Admiralty to build a larger screw-propelled steamer. Because the principle of the Archimedes screw was used in the design of this screw propeller, the ship was named the *Archimedes*. To implement Smith's patent, the Ship Propeller Company was founded. The *Archimedes* was built at Millwall on the Thames and launched in October 1838 as a three-masted top sail schooner. An 90 h.p. steam engine was used to drive her. After long trials, the original single screw was replaced by a double thread screw, with a diameter of 3,048 mm and a pitch of 3,048 mm, by means of which a speed of 9 knots was achieved. In 1840 the

Archimedes sailed round Great Britain and made the voyage to Oporto in Portugal in a record time. Thus she demonstrated successfully the ability of the screw propeller to drive a ship. After 1850 the *Archimedes* ended her career as a sailing ship running between Australia and Chile.

After the successful trials of the *Archimedes*, the three-masted barque *Novelty* was built in 1840 to be used in further experiments. The *Novelty* was provided with a 25 h.p. steam engine, her screw propeller was short and the shape of its blades were similar to those of a fan.

Dimensions of the *Archimedes*: length 106.5 feet (32.52 metres), beam 22.5 feet (6.86 metres), depth 13 feet (3.96 metres), deadweight 237 tons.

The *Great Britain* was the second ship designed by the naval architect Isambard Kingdom Brunel. She was built in the yard of W. Petterson and Sons in Bristol and launched in 1843. She was all-iron and, according to Brunel's specifications, she was provided with watertight transverse bulkheads. The ship had six masts with fore-and-aft rigging and a total sail surface area of 1,421 square metres. The cabins for the 360 passengers were all placed below deck. After the successful voyage of the *Archimedes* around Great Britain, Brunel decided to install a screw propeller instead of a paddle wheel. During her initial voyages in 1844, the *Great Britain* reached a speed of 11 knots, using a six-bladed, screw propeller driven by a steam engine. After this screw propeller was replaced by a four-bladed one, the speed of the ship was still further improved.

In February 1845 the ship was put on exhibition in London and in June of the same year she left Liverpool for New York, where she arrived in less than 15 days as the first all-iron ship. She was carrying 60 passengers and 806 tons of cargo. She continued to make journeys across the Atlantic until November 1846 when she was wrecked off the Irish coast. She was repaired and put into the Australian service. Thirty years later she was rebuilt and used for coal transport until 1937, when she was wrecked off the Falkland Islands. In the summer of 1970 she was towed back to Bristol, England, to be restored. Together with her sister ships, the *Great Western* and *Great Eastern*, which were built 15 years later, the *Great Britain* constituted an important development in shipbuilding in terms of design and propulsion.

Dimensions: length 289 feet (88.1 metres), beam 50.5 feet (15.4 metres), depth 32.5 feet (9.9 metres), displacement 3,270 tons.

The third and greatest ship built to the designs of the naval architect I.K. Brunel, was the *Leviathan*, renamed the *Great Eastern* when she was launched. In size and design she was forty years ahead of her time. The ship was intended to carry passengers and cargo from Europe to India and Australia and had to be economical over long distances. Construction was started in May 1854 at John Scott Russell and Co. in Millwall. The ship was all-iron and had four decks. The bottom and sides were of double cellular construction. The hull had a longitudinal system of framing and was subdivided by transverse bulkheads into twelve watertight compartments. The *Great Eastern* had five funnels and six masts with square and fore-and-aft rigging, with a sail surface area of about 6,500 square yards (5,435 square metres). The ship was designed to carry 4,000 passengers in three classes and 6,000 tons of cargo in addition to 12,200 tons of coal. The crew numbered 400.

The *Great Eastern* had paddle wheels at the sides, each with a diameter of 56 feet (17 metres) and 30 radial paddles and a four-bladed cast iron screw pro-

peller with a diameter of 24 feet (7.315 metres). The paddle wheels were driven by two steam engines which had a nominal output of 1000 h.p. The screw propeller was driven by a four-cylinder 1,622 h.p. steam engine. Steam was supplied by four double-ended tubular boilers.

The *Great Eastern* was launched on 31 January 1858 and her first voyage was to New York in 1860. She arrived after 11 days at sea and covered the distance at an average speed of 14 knots. However, because of the relatively small output of the engines and her paddle wheels, which were far too big and unsuitable for rough seas, the *Great Eastern* did not prove very successful either as a passenger or a cargo ship. In 1864 she was converted to a cable-laying ship, in 1885 taken out of service and was scrapped in 1888.

Dimensions: length between perps. 680 feet (207.26 metres), width of the hull 82.7 feet (25.21 metres), width over the paddle wheels 118 feet (36 metres), depth 48.2 feet (14.69 metres), draught 30 feet (9.15 metres), displacement 18,915 tons.

SCOTIA

The last and most elegant paddle wheeler of the Cunard company was the *Scotia*. She was built by Robert Napier and Sons at Govan as a two-masted brig and launched on 25 June 1861. The hull of the ship was made of iron and provided with six water-tight bulkheads. She had accommodation for 300 passengers and could carry 1400 tons of cargo. At the time of her launching the *Scotia* was considered the strongest ship on the seas. She was put into the Atlantic service in 1862. On her voyage from New York to Queenstown in 1863, covered in 8 days and 3 hours, she gained the speed record, which she held until 1867. The *Scotia* remained on the North Atlantic route as the last paddle steamer. After her last voyage in November 1875, she was sold to the Telegraph

Construction and Maintenance Co., who converted her to a twin-screw cable-laying ship.

An explosion took place on board in 1896 but thanks to the second collision bulkhead, it was possible to save her. In 1904 the *Scotia* was wrecked near Guam in the Ladrone Islands.

Dimensions: length o. a. 400 feet (121.9 metres), length between perps. 379 feet (115.8 metres), width of the hull 47.8 feet (14.6 metres), width over paddle boxes 76.5 feet (23.4 metres), depth of hold 30.5 feet (9.3 metres), draught 20 feet (6.1 metres), gross tonnage 3,871 tons, displacement 6,520 tons, nominal output of the side-lever engines 975 h.p. During conversion two-stage, expansion engines of 55 nominal h.p. were installed.

140

During the second half of the nineteenth century passenger transport between Europe and America steadily increased and the shipping companies tried to introduce larger, faster and better equipped passenger steamers. British companies maintained a primacy in this field both in terms of volume and speed of traffic. However in 1897 the German company, Norddeutscher Lloyd, put their new twin-propeller ship, the *Kaiser Wilhelm der Grosse*, into service on the Bremen, Southampton, New York route. On her first voyage she covered the distance between Southampton and New York in 5 days, 22 hours and 5 minutes, and thus achieved a speed of 21.39 knots. She even raised this to 22.33 knots on her subsequent voyages. Subsequently other German steamers, such as the *Deutschland* and the *Kronprinzessin Cecilie*, alternated in maintaining this record and it was only in 1907 that the Blue Ribbon of the Atlantic was recaptured by British ships.

The *Kaiser Wilhelm der Grosse* was built in the

Vulcan shipyard in Stettin. She was all-iron, had four decks, an overhanging forepost and an elliptical stern. The hull had a double bottom and was divided by 16 transverse bulkheads. A long superstructure with a sun deck, adjacent to the bridge, provided the passengers with a sheltered promenade. The ship had four funnels and two masts without sails. The cabins provided accommodation for 1,749 passengers. The crew numbered 450. The ship was driven by two three-stage, four-cylinder steam piston engines, which had a total output of 28,000 h.p. The steam needed for this was supplied by 13 boilers.

At the start of the First World War, the *Kaiser Wilhelm der Grosse* was equipped as an auxiliary cruiser and was later sunk by a British cruiser off the West African coast.

Dimensions: length 627.4 feet (191.2 metres), beam 66 feet (20.1 metres), depth 35.8 feet (10.9 metres), displacement 14,349 tons.

In 1897 the English inventor, Sir Charles Parsons, proved through his experimental ship, *Turbinia*, that steam turbines were suitable to drive ships. This led the Cunard Steamship Company to use steam turbines in their two new sister ships, the *Mauretania* and the *Lusitania*, which were designed to carry passengers and mail. Both ships were launched in 1906; the *Mauretania* was built by Swan Hunter and Wigham Richardson Ltd in Wallsend-on-Tyne and the *Lusitania* by John Brown and Company at Clydebank.

The hull of each ship had a double bottom, four continuous decks and was divided by 15 watertight bulkheads. The main superstructure, the promenade deck and the bridge, formed a single unit and occupied nearly the whole length of the ship. The *Mauretania* had cabin accommodation for 2,165 passengers in three classes. The crew numbered 812. The four four-bladed screw propellers, which were 16.8 feet (5.15 metres) in diameter, were driven directly by her steam turbines which developed in all some 70,925 h.p. The steam was supplied by 25 boilers.

At the end of 1907 both ships left on their maiden voyages from Liverpool to New York at an average speed of 23 knots and recaptured the Blue Ribbon for Great Britain. They held the record alternately until 1915 when the *Lusitania* was sunk by a German submarine. The *Mauretania* increased her speed to 25.9 knots and remained the holder of the Blue Ribbon until 1929, when the record was captured by the German ship, the *Bremen*.

During the First World War the *Mauretania* served initially as an auxiliary cruiser and later as a hospital ship. After the war she was again commissioned and in 1922 equipped with oil heating. In October 1934 the *Mauretania* was discarded and a year later sent to the scrapyard.

Dimensions: length 766.2 feet (232.32 metres), beam 88 feet (26.82 metres), depth 57.1 feet (17.4 metres), displacement 31,938 tons.

The first sea-going cargo ship to be provided with internal combustion engines was the *Selandia*, owned by the Danish East Asian Company. Together with her sister ship, *Fionia*, she was built in the shipyards of Burmeister and Wain in Copenhagen and designed to carry cargo and 26 passengers. The *Selandia* had a steel hull with a double bottom, two decks and six transverse bulkheads. The main deck carried two superstructures. Its two 125 h.p. Burmeister-Wain engines were a diesel type. They drove two screw propellers and were placed under the second superstructure in the stern. The *Selandia* had no funnel other than the mizzen mast (for exhaust gases). As well as the engine room, there were three holds in the hull. The diesel oil was stored in the double bottom.

The ship was commissioned in 1912. Except for the First World War when the *Selandia* served in the Pacific Ocean, she was in operation on the Copenhagen-Bangkok route until 1936. In that year she was sold to Norway and renamed the *Norseman*. In the period between 1938 and 1940 she was taken off active service because of severe damage, was later sold to the Finland America Line and after repairs hired by Japan as the *Tornator*. In 1942 she was wrecked in the bay of Omaisaki and sank. Her sister ship *Fionia* was sold to the Hamburg America Line soon after.

Dimensions: length 370.4 feet (112.9 metres), beam 53.2 feet (16.22 metres), depth 27.1 feet (8.26 metres), displacement 4,950 tons, cruising speed 11 knots.

The keel of the *Bremen*, owned by Norddeutscher Lloyd, was laid in Bremen, in the yards of the Deutsche Schiff und Maschinen Aktiengesellschaft in June 1927. The ship was launched on 6 August 1928. Compared with pre-war passenger ships, the *Bremen* and her sister ship, the *Europa*, showed many improvements in design and shape. The forepost was not upright but inclined towards the stern; the stern was similar to a cruiser's, whilst the deck superstructure was very compact. The *Bremen* had only two wide funnels, and her decks carried one hydroplane and a catapult. Altogether the *Bremen* had eleven decks, four of which were continuous ones running inside the hull, and four in the superstructures. The hull was subdivided by 14 watertight transverse bulkheads, which were fitted with hydraulic doors. The *Bremen* was equipped with every comfort to ease the life of her 2,224 passengers in four classes. The crew of the *Bremen* numbered 990.

Four four-bladed, screw propellers, five metres in diameter were driven by the steam turbines, which developed in all 125,000 h.p. Her twenty steam boilers were heated by oil. The *Bremen* won the Blue Ribbon on her maiden voyage from Bremerhaven via Southampton to New York in June 1929. She arrived in New York after 4 days, 14 hours and 42 minutes. In 1934 she further reduced her crossing time by three hours. Her average speed was 28 knots.

Before the beginning of the Second World War, the *Bremen* succeeded in running from New York and arrived safely in her home harbour of Bremen. In February 1941 she was hit in an air raid and destroyed by fire.

Dimensions: length 898.7 feet (273.92 metres), beam 101.9 feet (31.06 metres), depth 48.2 feet (14.69 metres), displacement 51,656 tons.

The *Normandie* is often held to be the most elegant passenger ship of the period before the Second World War. Her keel was laid in January 1931 in the yards of Chantiers et Ateliers de St Nazaire-Panhoët. She was launched in October 1932 and in May 1935 set out on her maiden voyage. Like the British *Queen Mary*, she was scheduled to sail every week between France and the U.S.A. She was owned by the Compagnie Générale Transatlantique.

The *Normandie* had a fine bow, a slightly overhanging stempost and an oval stern. Her double-bottom hull and five continuous decks were subdivided by 11 transverse bulkheads. The main deck almost covered the entire length of the ship. Above the main deck there was a long promenade deck and boat deck, adjoining the spacious, wide bridge. The third of her three funnels was just a dummy, which was added to complete the silhouette.

The ship was provided with modern fire-fighting equipment, life-saving equipment and the most up-to-date navigational aids. She was luxuriously appointed and had accommodation for 1,975 passengers in seven classes. The crew numbered 1,345.

Initially the *Normandie* was equipped with four three-bladed, screw propellers which were driven by a set of turbo-electric engines, which generated 160,000 h.p. The steam for these was produced by 29 tall pipe boilers, which were oil-heated. Using the original screw propeller the ship reached a maximum of 32.1 knots per hour during trials. In 1937 four-bladed propellers were installed and the *Normandie* won the Blue Ribbon on her voyage from New York to Europe which she covered in 3 days, 22 hours and 7 minutes at an average speed of 31.2 knots. During the war she was adopted by the United States and christened the *Lafayette*. During rebuilding as a troop-ship in February 1942, she caught fire and keeled over. In 1946 she was broken up.

Dimensions: length 981.5 feet (299.16 metres), beam 117.7 feet (35.88 metres), depth 91.8 feet (27.98 metres), gross tonnage 83,243 tons.

To provide a regular weekly link between Europe and America, the Cunard Steamship Company ordered a new passenger ship in the late 1920s. Construction began in August 1930 in the Clydebank shipyard of John Brown and Company Ltd. The world depression delayed the start by four years. In the meantime the Cunard and White Star Companies amalgamated and the British government decided to subsidise the building of the ship. The Queen Mary was launched in September 1934 and on 27 May 1936 she made her maiden voyage. She arrived in New York after 4 days and a mere 27 minutes. In 1938 she captured the Blue Ribbon, held at the time by the Normandie, when she made the crossing in 3 days, 20 hours and 42 minutes.

The Queen Mary had a rivetted shell and a transverse system of framing. The hull had a double bottom, five decks and, in accordance with the Convention of Safety of Life at Sea, was equipped with 15 watertight transverse bulkheads, which had hydraulic-

ally controlled sealing doors. The main deck, the promenade and sun decks were connected to the bridge and extended from the prow to the stern. The number of funnels was limited to three. The ship was designed for 2,139 passengers, accommodated in cabin, tourist and third classes. The crew numbered 1,101. The Queen Mary had four screw propellers, geared to four sets of turbines. Each set consisted of one high, two medium and one low pressure stage. The total output of 162,176 h.p. guaranteed the projected speed of 29 knots. The steam for the turbines was supplied by 24 water tube boilers, which were oil heated. During the Second World War, the Queen Mary was used as a troopship and was recommissioned on the North Atlantic run in 1947. In 1967 she was sold to the U.S.A. and anchored as a maritime museum in Long Beach, California.

Dimensions: length 975.2 feet (297.24 metres), beam 118.6 feet (36.15 metres), depth 68.5 feet (20.88 metres), gross tonnage 81,235 tons.

The *United States* has held the Blue Ribbon of the Atlantic since 1952; she gained this on her maiden voyage in July 1952 when she beat the record time set up by the *Queen Mary* in 1938. She topped the record on each crossing, that is from America to England and then back again; on the eastbound journey she averaged a speed of 35.59 knots and on the westbound voyage a speed of 34.51 knots; in so doing she cut down the time for the Atlantic crossing by four days. She remained in service until 1969 when she was withdrawn for economic reasons.

The *United States* was built in a record time in the Newport News shipyard in Virginia; her keel was laid in February 1950 and she was launched as early as June 1951. Her main features include a slightly inclined forepost, a cruiser's stern and two long, continuous superstructures, which are neatly connected to the navigation bridge. Her two broad funnels have smoke wings and her promenade deck separates the steel hull from the main superstructures; all of which, except for the forecastle, are made out of light alloys. The interior equipment and furniture are almost exclusively made out of fireproof material.

The *United States* can accommodate 2,008 passengers in three classes and, in addition, can carry 4,191 cubic metres of general cargo and 1,359 cubic metres of refrigerated cargo in her holds. The crew numbers 1,093. The ship was originally built as a passenger liner but may be converted into a troopship, capable of carrying 14,000 men. The ship has facilities to provide for all the creature comforts of passengers; these include saloons, bars, a cinema, swimming pool, and nursery.

The four screw propellers are driven by four Westinghouse Electric Corp. steam turbines and have a maximum output of 240,000 h.p. Steam is supplied by eight Babcock and Wilcox boilers, which are oil-fired.

Dimensions: length o.a. 990 feet (301.8 metres), beam 101.6 feet (30.97 metres), draught 36 feet (10.98 metres), displacement 56,000 tons.

The *France* is one of the most recent and largest passenger ships. Her overall length of 1,035 feet (315.66 metres) makes her the longest liner in the world. Her keel was laid in October 1957 in the yards of the Chantiers de l'Atlantique in St Nazaire for the Compagnie Générale Transatlantique. She was launched in May 1960 and finally finished in the autumn of 1961. During trials in November 1961 she reached a maximum speed of 34 knots and completed a successful maiden voyage to New York in February 1962. She is scheduled to maintain a weekly service between France and the U.S.A. on the North Atlantic route.

In concept the *France* is similar to the *United States*. She is entirely welded, her superstructure is made of light alloys, her hull has a double bottom and four continuous decks. Under the terms of the 1948 International Convention she is subdivided by 15 watertight bulkheads, which have hydraulically remote-controlled doors. Her superstructure is continuous, runs the entire length of the ship and links up with the bridge. Her two aerodynamic funnels have side wings so that the smoke is directed sideways and the deck is protected from falls of soot.

The *France* can accommodate 2,044 passengers, of which 407 are first class and 1,637 are tourist class. The crew numbers 1,000. She has four, simply geared screw propellers, which are driven by four steam turbines with a total output of 160,000 h.p. Steam is supplied by eight steep tube boilers, fired by oil. She has two pairs of Denny Brown stabilisers.

Dimensions: length o.a. 1,034.9 feet (315.66 metres), beam moulded 110.5 feet (33.70 metres), depth to the promenade deck 92 feet (28.1 metres), displacement 58,000 tons.

THE PASSENGER SHIP *MICHELANGELO*

The *Michelangelo* was built in the Ansaldo shipyards in 1965 and along with her sister ship, the *Raffaelo*, which was constructed in the yards of the Cantieri Riuniti del Adriatico in Trieste, she is one of the largest and most beautiful liners in the world. Both ships were commissioned by the Italian Line Shipping Company and put into service on the North American, Mediterranean route. The hull of the ship is all welded, she has eleven decks and in line with the International Convention (SOLAS) of 1960, her hull is subdivided by watertight bulkheads, which have remote-controlled doors. To reduce weight her superstructure is made of aluminium alloys. The funnels are cased in an outer lattice structure, at the top of which there are side wings to prevent smuts falling on to the deck. Propulsion is provided by two screw propellers, which are driven by two two-phase steam turbines, made by Ansaldo and generating a total of 86,000 h.p. Steam is supplied by four Foster Wheeler boilers, which produce 149,000 lb. pressure per hour. The ship can accommodate 1,829 passengers in three classes. There is a cinema for 500 people, six swimming pools, clubs and recreation rooms. The crew numbers 720. The hold can accommodate 40 cars.

The ship has a fire-fighting system, air-conditioning and other safety systems. Television equipment keeps a permanent watch on the action of the screw propellers and the rudder. The maximum speed of the vessel in 29 knots and her cruising speed 26.5 knots.

Dimensions: length o.a. 900.5 feet (275.5 metres), beam 101.75 feet (31 metres), depth 51.6 feet (15.75 metres), draught 30.3 feet (9.25 metres), deadweight 49,900 tons.

QUEEN ELIZABETH II

After trials and certain modifications the *Queen Elizabeth II* was commissioned in December 1968. She is the most efficient merchantman in the world and the second largest passenger ship built by Britain. The *Queen Elizabeth II* was built in the Clydebank shipyard of Upper Clyde Shipbuilders Ltd, formerly John Brown's, where her two famous predecessors, the *Queen Mary* and the *Queen Elizabeth* were built. Her owners, the Cunard Company, anticipate that she will be used for fast travel along the North Atlantic routes and also for sea cruises.

The ship has an oblique, arch-shaped stempost with a bulbous bow and cruiser's stern; she has a compact superstructure and a great area of deck space. Her modern, tubular, single mast towers over the wide navigation bridge; her funnel has a wind scoop and is situated aft; her hull is made of steel and entirely welded, and her superstructure, also welded, is made of light alloys. She has 13 decks, and carries

the same number of passengers as the earlier 'Queens' but has a smaller draught and displacement. Her 2,025 passengers are accommodated in two classes; seventy-five per cent of the cabins directly overlook the sea. The crew numbers 906, which is about one third less than that of the preceding Cunard ships.

Her two six-bladed, screw propellers are driven by two Brown Pametrada steam turbines with a total output of 110,000 h.p. Steam is provided by three giant Foster Wheeler boilers with oil burning. For better manoeuvring in ports a bow jet propeller is provided. The most up-to-date navigational aids and one computer for evaluating and checking her operation have been installed.

Dimensions: length o.a. 963 feet (293.7 metres), beam 105 feet (32 metres), draught 36.5 feet (11.1 metres), deadweight 60,000 tons, cruising speed 28.5 knots.

Smaller sailing or motor yachts are mainly used for sport and pleasure in coastal waters, although in the course of time motor yachts have been developed for long-distance sea voyages and larger numbers of passengers. They are made entirely of steel and displace 150 to 200 tons or more. Their equipment includes such modern navigational aids as gyropilots, echo-sounders and radar. Modern machinery, stabilisers, air conditioning, water plant, refrigerators etc., provide for the faultless operation of the ship and the maximum comfort of the passengers. The shape of such ships is determined by the most famous naval architects of the day on the basis of model trials, so that the yacht, in appearance, is one of the most elegant of vessels. They have one or two screw propellers, usually driven by oil engines with a total output up to 1,000 h.p., which gives them a speed of 12 to 15 knots and more. The cabins may have their own bathrooms, whilst saloons, studies, messes and other rooms may be provided according to the design of the craft. Motor yachts are owned by rich private people, statesmen, organisations and royal families.

One of the best known and largest motor yachts is the British Royal Yacht *Britannia*, built in 1954 in the Clydebank shipyards of John Brown Ltd. She was built as a multi-purpose craft; in peace time she can be used by the royal family and during war she can become a hospital ship. Her deadweight is 5,769 tons. Two steam turbines generating 12,000 h.p. give her a speed of 21 knots. The tradition of British royal yachts goes back a thousand years, although the first recorded mention of these ships dates from the beginning of the seventeenth century. The first royal yacht, the *Mary*, was built in 1660 for Charles II, although where it was built is not known.

Ship architects are continually trying to increase the speed of ships. One of the ways is to reduce the resistance of the ship's hull in the water. Wings with an aerodynamic profile, placed under the hull, make the ship rise above the surface when a certain speed is reached and due to the ensuing dynamic displacement, the ship's resistance is substantially reduced. The first trials with wing boats, or hydrofoils, were carried out as early as the beginning of this century. Further developments took place in the years before the Second World War and after that in the fifties, when the Swiss firm of Supramar and the Soviet Union began to build hydrofoils of various types and sizes, individually and then in series.

The shape and arrangement of the wings vary according to the specific design. The wings can be arranged under the ship's bottom in the form of a V or located individually at the sides of the ship or even under the stern as fixed, folding or even revolvable ones. The screw propellers are usually driven by diesel engines or gas turbines with a high output. The speed of hydrofoils is 70 to 130 km per hour. To save weight, the hull of a wing boat is usually made of light alloys.

Hydrofoils are used for local and long-distance transport on rivers, lakes, bays and straits, such as in the Finnish Gulf, in the Strait of Messina in the Adriatic sea, the straits of the Japanese sea etc. They may carry up to 150 passengers. The best-known hydrofoils are the product of the Supramar firm, the series PT 10, 20, 50, 150, the American Denison boats and Soviet ships of the 'Volga', 'Raketa', 'Meteor', 'Kometa', 'Tschajka' and 'Burevestnik' classes.

The Supramar type, PT 50 is 91.16 feet (27.8 metres) long and capable of carrying 90 passengers. Two diesel engines with a total output of 2,700 h.p. give the ship a speed of 41 knots (75 km) per hour. The boats are produced under licence in Italy, Finland and Japan.

The principle of the hovercraft, that is movement by means of an air cushion, created by a system of fans between the ship's bottom and the water surface, has hitherto been mainly applied to water transport. From the first trials in the second half of the fifties and in the course of the next ten years, the production of hovercraft became an industry dominated by Great Britain. Every builder solves the shape, the arrangement of the air ducts and the flexible skirts in different way. The fans are usually driven by diesel engines or gas turbines. Forward motion is made possible by air propellers with adjustable blades, driven either directly by the engines or geared to the engines driving the fans. British firms, such as Hovermarine Ltd., Vosper Ltd., Vickers Armstrong Ltd., and Westland Aircraft have been involved in the development of the hovercraft.

The greatest hovercraft built to date is the SRN4 of the 'Mountbatten' class, built by the British Hovercraft Corporation Ltd. She is designed to carry passengers and vehicles over short distances and over water whose waves do not exceed a height of 10 feet. The hovercraft can travel over water and land. She has side doors for the passengers and loading gates fore and aft for vehicles. The SRN4 can carry either 609 seated passengers or 174 passengers and 34 vehicles. In calm weather she can carry 63.5 tons of cargo at a maximum speed of 70 knots. Her fans and screw propellers are driven by four Rolls Royce, Marine Proteus gas turbines, which generate 3,400 h.p. each. The hovercraft SRN4, was commissioned in April 1969 to ply between Dover and Boulogne.

Dimensions: length o.a. on landing pads 130 feet 2 inches (39.7 metres), beam moulded 78 feet (23.8 metres), overall height 36 feet 2 inches (11 metres), cruising speed 40 – 50 knots.

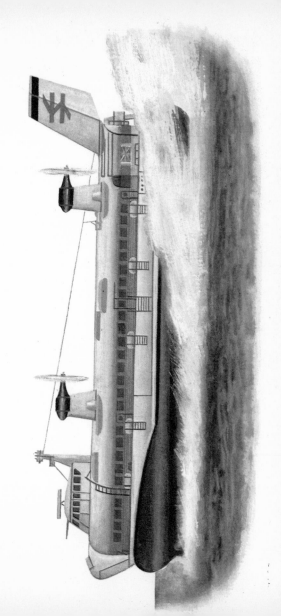

For sport and pleasure as well as for fishing in coastal waters, motor cruisers are built. Wood, steel, aluminium alloys and recently plastics, such as laminated glassfibre, are used for the construction of the hull. The design of the hull is usually arrived at after trials with models, intended to decrease resistance and give the yachts greater speed. Usually the underwater section of the hull is V-shaped. The sunken cabin is usually, in the fore part of the ship and is equipped for long stays at sea, with berths, gas or paraffin stoves, heating, refrigerators, etc. The cabin is connected to the raised, steering cockpit, which gives a good view over the bow. Larger types of motor cruisers have their accommodation amidships and an open steering platform above. Such cruisers are equipped with such modern navigational aids as echo-sounders, speedometers, radio and radar. A short mast with navigation lights projects above the steering house. The stern of the yacht is usually uncovered or partly covered, providing a space for possible fishing for which special inclinable fishing rods are available. In such motor cruisers the accommodation is generally for four to six people.

The yachts are driven either by inboard engines, geared to one or two screw propellers or by one to three outboard motors. Their total output can be 300 h.p. or more. Their maximum speed is usually about 40 knots.

The area of the Great Lakes on the border between Canada and the U.S.A. is particularly suited to intensive passenger and cargo shipping. Ships maintain a steady traffic between the main industrial centres such as Chicago, Milwaukee, Green Bay, Duluth, Detroit, Cleveland and Toronto. The construction of the St Lawrence Seaway in 1958 linked this region with the Atlantic and opened up navigational communications with the entire world.

Corn, iron and aluminium ores, oil and industrial goods in this area are the main cargoes on the Great Lakes. In the course of time, the Great Lakes cargo ships involved in this trade have assumed a typical shape and appearance. The engine room, the superstructure and the funnel are situated aft, and the bow carries the commander's bridge. The ships have no cargo-handling equipment of their own since the harbours they visit have all the necessary facilities in the way of cranes, grabs, elevators etc. The ships are laid out according to the type of cargo to be carried, be it general, bulk or liquid cargo.

The hull is made of welded steel, although occasionally it might be still partly rivetted; the bow is short and rising; the superstructure is made of aluminium alloys and the ship usually has a single screw propeller, driven by a diesel engine. Great Lakes ships reach a length of 730 feet (222.5 metres), have a beam of 75 feet (23 metres) and have a deadweight capacity around 24,000 tons. Recent developments include the introduction of remote control and the automisation of the ship to increase safety and reduce the number of the crew.

Coasters are a varied assortment of cargo ships designed to carry goods along the coast from one harbour to another, eventually to operate in the estuaries of great rivers. They may be bulk carrier general cargo ships, refrigerated vessels, tankers or specially designed ships such as container carriers. They weigh between 1,000 and 3,000 tons. Their engine room is located amidships or, in recent models, more often aft. For navigation on the open sea they have a relatively high bow, which gives them, along with their distinctive stern superstructure and funnel, a characteristic appearance. They are fitted out with their own loading and unloading equipment to make them independent of their ports of call.

In appearance and size coasters resemble combined river and sea-going ships, and their shallow draught

allows them to sail up rivers and reach inland harbours.

An example of a modern coaster is the Dutch *Unden*, which was built in the C. Amels and Son shipyards in Makkum for N.V. Romulus of Amsterdam. The *Unden* is designed to carry timber and rolls of paper from Sweden to Holland. She has extremely powerful loading equipment, which enables her to unload within a day. Her hatch covers are hydraulically controlled. Her single four-bladed screw propeller is driven by a 1500 h.p. MaK diesel engine which gives her a maximum speed of 12.4 knots.

Dimensions: length o.a. 254 feet (77.66 metres), beam 38.9 feet (11.85 metres), draught 13.5 feet (4.14 metres), displacement 1,639 tons.

Sea-going cargo ships are diesel or steam-driven vessels designed for carrying dry or liquid cargoes. They can carry up to twelve passengers but if they carry more they are classified as mixed ships and regulated as such by the international rules and conventions governing passenger transport.

The main types of dry cargo ships are the bulk and general cargo carriers. The transverse bulkheads of such vessels divide the hull into individual holds, whose hatchways are fitted with covers of various designs, including sliding or folding ones, which are electrically or electrohydraulically controlled. Cargo derricks and booms, cranes and conveyors are on board for purposes of loading and unloading cargo. The booms are inclined, revolvable and adjoined to masts of various types, such as column, dipod, tripod, portal and other masts.

The vessels are entirely steel-built, normally welded, have one or two screw propellers and are driven by oil, steam engines or steam turbines. An indication of the normal engine type is given by the fact that some 65 % of the world's merchant fleet has diesel propulsion. Modern navigational instruments and automatic machinery ensures safety and easy control of these vessels. Their deadweight ranges from 5,000 to 30,000 tons and their average speed from 15 to 20 knots.

Bulk cargo ships specialise in carrying coal, metal ores, grain, sugar, and fertilisers and similarly general cargo ships are usually designed specifically to take a particular cargo, such as locomotives, cars, rolls of paper, bags, bales, cases, containers, timber or refrigerated goods.

THE NUCLEAR SHIP *SAVANNAH*

In 1956 the United States Congress decided to build the first nuclear-powered commercial ship. The keel was laid in 1958 in the yards of the New York Shipbuilding Corporation in Camden. The *Savannah* is a mixed ship, carrying cargo and passengers and was built as an experimental craft by the U.S. Maritime Administration and the Atomic Energy Commission. She was launched on 21 July 1959 and commissioned for a trial period in 1960.

The *Savannah* has a shelter deck, a clipper bow and a cruiser stern. The bridge is connected to the three-deck superstructure which has no funnel and is situated in the after part of the ship. The cabins for 60 passengers are situated in the forward section of this superstructure. The crew numbers 110; the holds can take 9,500 tons of cargo, and the ship was designed to travel at 21 knots and be capable of staying at sea for 300,000 miles.

The two-phase, geared screw propeller is driven by a De Laval steam turbine and has a nominal output of 20,272 h.p. Steam is supplied by two steam generators, which are heated by the cooling water used with the atomic reactor. The reactor was built by Babcock and Wilcox and has a nominal potential of 74 mw. The fuel is enriched U 235 and the reactor and both generators are housed in a steel pressure chamber.

After long delays caused by conflicts between the owners and the trade unions, the *Savannah* finally left on a series of voyages, but the results of tests carried out then could not be used because in the ensuing interval her atomic reactor had become obsolete.

Dimensions: length 595.5 feet (175.71 metres), beam 78.17 feet (23.85 metres), depth 29.58 feet (9.03 metres), gross tonnage 10,190 tons.

THE GIANT OIL-TANKER *UNIVERSE KOREA*

The construction of giant oil-tankers began in Japan at the beginning of the 1960s in the SASEBO and Ishikawajima Harima Heavy Industries shipyards. Among the largest oil-tankers in the world are the *Universe Ireland*, the *Universe Kuwait* and the *Universe Korea*. They are sister ships and three of a series of six ordered by National Bulk Carriers Inc. of the U.S.A. from the firms of IHI and SASEBO. They are under longterm contracts with the Gulf Oil Corporation and carry oil from Kuwait to Ireland via Capetown. In Ireland the oil is pumped into 50,000-ton tankers and redirected into European refineries.

The keel of the first ship in the series was laid in October 1967 and the vessel launched in March 1968. After successful trials she was handed over to her owners in September 1968.

The ships are built with massive transverse systems of framing and in addition to the transverse bulkheads they have two longitudinal ones. The engine room and the superstructure are located aft of the ship. The exhaust gases are led off by two funnels, placed side by side. The continuous bridge, which is typical of tankers, runs from the aft to fore amidships. The ships have two five-bladed screw propellers which are 23.6 feet in diameter. Two steam turbines made by IHI General Electrics, generate a total of 37,400 h.p. and provide the necessary drive. Steam is supplied by two IHI-Foster Wheeler boilers, which produce 150 tons per hour. The cruising speed is 14.6 knots. All principal gear and piping systems are installed in duplicate and the pumping of oil and ballast water is central operated and remote controlled. The crew numbers a mere 76.

Dimensions: length o.a. 1,132.8 feet (345.3 metres), length between perps. 1,082.7 feet (330 metres), beam 174.9 feet (53.3 metres), depth 105 feet (32 metres), draught full-loaded 81.5 feet (24.8 metres), deadweight capacity 326,585 tons, cargo oil tanks' capacity 399,630 cubic metres.

Container ships are a sophisticated type of cargo ship, used for carrying general cargo; their holds and handling equipment are adapted to deal with very large containers of internationally standardised dimensions. The design, size and layout of the hatchways correspond to the size and shape of the containers; the walls of the holds are vertical and thus allow the maximum use of space by the containers. To facilitate loading and unloading the vessels normally have loading bays in the sides at the stern or in the prow.

The result of such arrangements is to give the container ships a distinctive appearance, as for example the location of the superstructure housing the engine room in the after part of the vessel. Other features include the simple, angular shape of the hull with its transom stern, the deck without any cargo derricks or masts and the stern and side loading ports. Their speed is generally in excess of 20 knots and their deadweight between 10,000 and 15,000 tons. It is only comparatively recently that countries with an advanced shipbuilding industry began building container ships and the roll-on, roll-off or RO-RO ships are even more recent. Piers and harbours have had to be suitably adapted to load and unload container ships to ensure quick and economic handling of cargo.

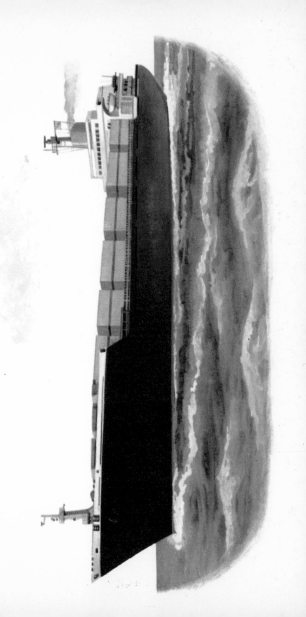

Ferries are used to carry passengers, trains and motor vehicles over short stretches of water. The hold of a railway ferryboat has between two and four sets of rails and when the destination is reached the moulded part of the stern section opens and the rails are coupled to the railway lines on the land. On ferries used to convey motor vehicles, there is usually more than one storage deck and the remainder of the high superstructure is used as saloons and restaurants for passengers during the voyage.

To facilitate manoeuvres in harbour, ferries usually have two screw propellers and in the forward part of the vessel a further auxiliary steering device, located below the waterline and which can take the form of a Voith-Schneider or submerged bow jet propeller. Such ferries can travel at 20 knots and can carry up to 20 express railway coaches or a large number of motor cars.

Ferryboats are used extensively between Britain and Europe, between the Danish islands and Scandinavia, on the Baltic Sea and the Great Lakes of North America and in Japan.

One of the fastest ferryboats is the Swedish *Stena Germanica*, which operates between Kiel in Germany and Gothenburg in Sweden. She has two MAN engines, capable of 8,640 h.p., she can travel at a speed of 23.5 knots and can carry 1,400 passengers and 200 motor vehicles.

Lifeboats (or rescue cruisers) are special craft designed for the quick rescue of the crews and passengers of wrecked ships. They are solidly built steel vessels provided with air chambers which make them nearly unsinkable. Lifeboats are equipped with all types of rescue devices, such as life jackets, rings and rafts, apparatus for tossing a line, saving sails, oil for calming the waves, hand pumps, powerful loudspeakers etc. Their equipment also includes respirators, fire pumps and an efficient radio set. In Britain, lifeboat crews are made up of trained members of the Royal National Lifeboat Institution, which was founded as early as 1824.

Lifeboats are of two basic types: a smaller type ready for action in certain coastal areas and larger boats, provided with powerful engines, which patrol the dangerous waters of the open sea.

A harbour tug has to carry out various towing duties in harbours and river estuaries, such as towing cargo ships and liners to boarding and unloading quays, docks and shipyards and from harbours out to the open sea. Sometimes they are used for salvage work in harbours, as in cases of fire. For this they are equipped with powerful pumps and water guns, which are placed on their raised bridge or on the special tower-mast. If used as icebreakers their shell is strengthened and they have a spoon bow and possibly ballast tanks. The harbour tugs have a raised bow and a relatively high superstructure, housing the bridge, which is positioned towards the bow to obtain better visibility.

Ships are towed by ropes, one end of which is fixed to the towing hook of the tug behind the funnel; the other end is fixed to the bollards of the towed ship. The towing hook is revolvable, cushioned and often provided with fast-acting release gear. The afterdeck has several towing bows, along which the towing rope slides. The bow, stern and sides of the tug are protected against the chocks by woven or rubber buffers. Harbour tugs are also equipped with powerful engines and to gain better manoeuvrability they sometimes have their propellers in Kort nozzles or are fitted with the Voith-Schneider propeller.

THE PUSHER-TUG *UNITED STATES*

Before and after the Second World War trials were carried out with a new towing system, called pushing, on the rivers of America and Europe. The technique involves the pusher-tug pushing a group of closely connected barges, one behind the other. Of course the tug is specially adapted for this purpose; she is short, has a high superstructure and steering house, excellent steering gear and coupling devices for linking up the barges and in her bow she has special pushing poles. Pushing has proved its value on the waterways of America and Europe.

The most powerful pusher-tug in service is the *United States*, which plies between St Louis and New Orleans on the lower reaches of the Mississippi, pushing the barges of the Federal Barge Lines Incorporated. She was built in the dockyard of the St Louis Shipbuilding and Steel Company and launched in December 1958.

The *United States* has a totally welded, steel body, which cuts the waterline at an angle. She has a raised stern and a massive three-deck superstructure, which contains the steering house, the crew's quarters, galley, messes and recreation rooms. This tug can push at least 40 barges, which gives it a total length of 1750 feet (533 metres) and a surface area of six acres. She is driven by four diesel engines capable of generating 8,616 h.p. Her screw propellers have a diameter of 2,743 mm and are enclosed in Kort nozzles. The vessel has four rudders of which two are fore and two aft.

Dimensions: length 180 feet (54.9 metres), beam 58 feet (17.7 metres), draught 12.6 feet (3.85 metres), displacement 2,086 tons. Her speed varies according to the number of barges being pushed and ranges from 7 to 15 miles per hour (13–28 km per hour).

The name 'cutter' is applied either to small, single-masted ships, which are fore-and-aft rigged with one gaff main sail, one topsail and 2 to 3 focs, or for a larger rowing boat with 2 masts and gaff sails, which is used as an auxiliary boat of a warship or for the training of sailors. Fishing cutters are small, wooden, steel or composite motor vessels, which are used for trawling in coastal waters or on the open sea. They have auxiliary rigging which usually consists of two masts, set with long-and-aft sails. They are stoutly built and vary in length from between 39 to 66 feet. The stern deck houses the wheel house and the engine room, the crew is accommodated in the bow, whilst admidships are the holds to take the fish. The spartan facilities of the ship are related to the short stays at sea and such vessels are usually manned by a crew of six to seven men. The ship has a diesel engine of between 65 to 135 h.p. driving the single propeller, which is often equipped with adjustable blades. The speeds reached by a fishing cutter vary between 8 and 10 knots.

At present, fishing cutters are the smallest and the most numerous type of fishing craft. They trawl in the fishing grounds of the North, Baltic and Mediterranean Seas and the Atlantic seaboard and thus ensure a regular supply of fish for the markets of European harbour towns. The specifications of their design often differ according to their area of operation and fishing techniques employed.

A larger type of fishing vessel, similar to cutters, is the lugger, which has a far greater storage capacity of between 100 and 150 tons. They spend a much longer time at sea and therefore have a larger crew and refrigerated holds.

The trawler is a fishing vessel designed for fishing on the open sea, using trawls in association with drift nets. According to the way in which the nets are hauled and the fish lifted on to the deck, trawlers are distinguished as side trawlers, which have gallows projecting on their sides, or stern trawlers, which have a sloping ramp in the stern, enclosed by a gate. The ropes of the nets are coiled in over a series of pulleys located on the gallows or the gate, by a powerful winch. When the net is lifted on deck, it is opened and the fish is sorted and stored in refrigerated holds, or is salted in barrels, or is immediately transformed into fish flour, oil and fillets, or is cut up into portions and canned. If this is the case the trawler will have its own cooling and refrigerating system. As a result trawlers, which were originally small,

steam-driven ships with simple holds, have developed into modern, floating fish factories. They are powered by diesel or diesel electric engines or steam turbines with oil-fired boilers. Their screw propellers usually have adjustable blades or function in rotating Kort nozzles to give the ship more manoeuvrability. Modern trawlers have the requisite facilities for long stays at sea in the coarse fishing grounds of the Northern and Southern Atlantic. They have electronic and acoustic devices to find and determine the movements of shoals of fish. The size of the trawler is determined by the distance of the fishing ground from the home port. Side trawlers reach a deadweight capacity of 1,000 tons, whilst stern trawlers range from 2,500 tons to 3,000 tons.

It is more than fifty years since the last whaling sailing ships ploughed the oceans of the northern and southern hemispheres. Their crews were made up of brave and hardened men who hunted whales individually on board slender, fast whaleboats and subsequently processed themselves the catch on board their mother ships, transforming the whale meat into oil. Today their work has been taken over by whale catchers, which are similar to large trawlers and have high prows on which are located the harpoon guns. A catwalk links this prow to the bridge, and the crow's nest on top of a tall mast enables the movement of whales to be closely followed. The caught whales are inflated with compressed air and towed alongside the ship to the whaling factory ship or are slowly processed on board the whale catcher itself.

The stern of a whaling factory ship has a slipway, up which the whales are hauled. Then the layers of blubber are peeled away and melted down in boilers, while the meat is tinned or turned into fish flour. These ships are equipped with everything necessary for a stay of several months at sea. Each of them is a floating base for eight to ten whale catchers. Such factory ships are owned by the great fishing companies and have a deadweight of between 30,000 and 40,000 tons. The Norwegians pioneered the processing of fish at sea and first opened up the Antarctic fishing grounds. The tremendous advances in fishing brought about by the introduction of factory ships began before the Second World War and has continued up to the present. Currently fleets of factory ships are owned by Norway, Japan, Great Britain, the Soviet Union, Germany, South Africa and Argentina.

Icebreakers are used to keep waterways free and open in the northern oceanic areas and the polar seas. They are vessels of formidable power whose hulls are adapted to break up continuous pack ice. The bow is spoon-shaped to enable the ship virtually to ride up on the ice and the midship section is wedge-shaped so that the masses of ice cannot push vertically towards the hull. The shell of the vessel is strengthened, especially in the bow and along the waterline and the ballast tanks are housed in the hull. It is possible to pump water from one of these tanks to another and so create the rolling movement which assists in breaking up the ice. Icebreakers used in areas of continuous but not necessarily thick sheets of ice have sometimes an additional screw propeller under the overhanging bow whose wake leads off the broken blocks of ice. Polar icebreakers can break up ice up to six metres thick, although the average icebreaker is used for ice two metres thick.

In 1960 the Soviet atomic icebreaker *Lenin* was

commissioned for use in the Arctic area and was the first surface ship in the world with atomic propulsion. She has three stern screw propellers driven by three turbine engines with an output of 44,000 h.p. Steam is supplied by three independent nuclear reactors, which are cooled by pressurised water and situated amidships, where they are housed in a specially insulated area which has walls 420 mm thick. The resistance and structure of the hull and the number of bulkheads are in accordance with the regulations laid down by the International Convention of 1948. Her speed is 18 knots in free water and 2 knots when breaking up ice 2.4 metres thick. The *Lenin* has extended the period when shipping is possible in the northern ice zone from two to four months.

Dimensions: length o.a. 439.3 feet (134 metres), beam moulded 90.5 feet (27.6 metres), depth 52.8 feet (16.1 metres), draught 30.2 feet (9.2 metres), displacement 16,000 tons.

SALVAGE VESSEL

Salvage vessels are sometimes purpose-built but more often they are large ships that have been rebuilt from passenger or cargo vessels. An example of the former type are the double-hulled ships that were built shortly after the First World War to lift sunken submarines. Salvage vessels normally have powerful cranes and winches, caissons, oxyacetylene cutting equipment for use underwater, powerful pumps for work on sunken craft, ventilation fans and special devices to produce chemicals to make a wreck float.

Such ships have their own repair shops on board for repairing ship's machinery and quarters for the divers who are needed for underwater salvage work. Powerful tugs, like harbour and sea-going tugs, are used to tow away the damaged craft to be salvaged and they are equipped with fire fighting pumps for emergency use. Salvage ships are used by most fleets in the great maritime countries, especially those of Great Britain, the U.S.A., France, Germany, the U.S.S.R., the Netherlands and Poland.

CABLE-LAYING SHIP

The cable-laying ship is another special type of sea-going vessel, which is used for laying, checking and repairing submarine cables. Circular tanks are housed in the hull of the vessel where several thousand kilometres of cable are carefully coiled together. The cable is drawn out of these tanks by a special winch and spool system and is then led over a series of rollers to a huge guide pulley located on an outrigger overhanging the bow. The cable slides into the water over this pulley. The largest cable-laying ships often have a cable winch and the appropriate main pulley, which is found on the stern deck. In addition to engines, pumps and piping systems, these vessels also have workshops for the repair of cables and quality control shops where they conduct continual tests on the cable's insulation, conductivity and other features, vital to the laying of the cable on the seabed.

The first ships used for laying deep cable were the English ship-of-the-line *Agamemnon* and the American *Niagara* as long ago as 1858. The greatest ship of the nineteenth century, the *Great Eastern*, was also used for cable-laying after she had been rebuilt. Today, cable-laying ships are owned by all the great maritime nations, through their telegraphic and postal organisations, which control their appropriate section of the intercontinental, telegraphic communications system or have their own cable communications network. The most up-to-date cable-laying ships include the Canadian *John Cabot* built in 1965, the British *Alert* and *Ocean Layer, Long Lines* of 1961, the American *John Cabot* built in 1965, the Soviet *Ingul* and *Jana* of 1963. Modern cable-laying ships are usually powered by electric diesel engines as these increase their manoeuvrability.

Research ships are special craft which study, record and measure the seas and oceans. Their investigations include the movement and nature of sea currents, an analysis of sea salts, life at sea, the distinctive water layers and the depth of the sea in specific areas. They explore and analyse the composition of the seabed and in so doing provide data for oceanic cartography, the extraction of the mineral and oil wealth of the sea, for the location of fishing grounds and the appropriateness of fishing techniques and for determining the geodetic and other natural features of the seabed. Research ships have nautical and special measuring apparatus, and winches capable of lowering depth anchors and sound recording instruments to a great depth. They also carry a wide range of technical equipment, such as nets for collecting plankton, diving gear and bells, underwater photographic, cinematographic and television cameras. A range of laboratories are found on board where the results of primary research can be evaluated by further instruments and computers. Research ships usually have equipment to neutralise vibrations and the rolling of the ships; they are easily manoeuvrable, have sound-proof areas and are air-conditioned throughout.

The most important research ships include the German *Meteor* built in 1965, the French *Triton*, the Soviet *Academician Lomonosov* and *Zarja*, which is a ship used for measuring the earth's magnetism, the American *John Biscoe*, which operates in the polar regions, the *Carnegie*, *Galilei* and others. Ships involved in the famous polar expeditions at the dawn of the twentieth century were also equipped as research vessels and included Nansen's *Fram*, Scott's *Discovery* and *Terra Nova* and Charcot's *Pourquoi-pas*.

LIGHTSHIP

The lightship is a distinctive vessel performing the same function as a lighthouse, namely to ensure the safety of shipping in the vicinity of cliffs, coastal straits and shallow waters, in river estuaries and the entrance to harbours. The ship is very stoutly built and has a massive, tower-shaped mast that carries a light on its top. In addition to light signals, lightships can also sound fog alarms and are fitted out with radio transmitters and receivers.

Lightships are anchored in the spot where they operate and, in the event of a storm and the consequent need to release this anchorage, they sometimes have their own propulsion, although generally this is not the case. Normally, they are towed out to their destination by tugs or special auxiliary craft, called lighthouse tenders, which also supply them with regular provisions. Some lightships in fact have no crew at all and are fully automatic.

Lightships are painted in various colours according to their nationality and anchorage. They are found anchored off the Thames estuary (the *Sunk*), the Firth of Forth (the *North Carr*) and in the estuary of the Elbe (the *Elbe* I to IV and the *Borkumriff*). Recently, however, efforts have been made to replace lightships by permanent lighthouses for economic reasons.

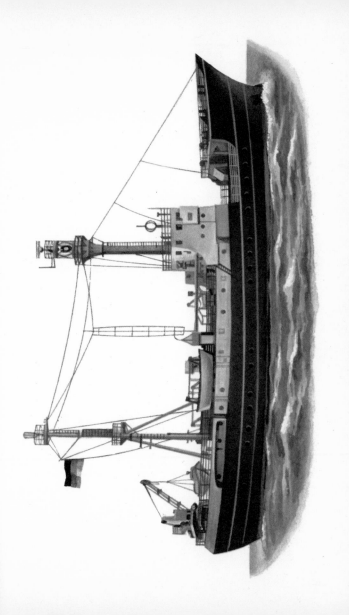

SEA HOPPER-DREDGER

Floating dredgers belong to the group of engineering craft. Dependent upon the type of dredging system being used, they are classified into bucket, suction, grab, dipper, rake and polyp dredgers. The dredged soil is carried to the shore by pipes, conveyors or prams. Sea hoppers that operate as suction dredgers in harbours, river estuaries, bays and channels have their own holds, are self-propelled and are therefore capable of unloading the dredged soil in a suitable place.

Their equipment consists of a revolving section head, suction pipe, centrifugal pump and a discharge pipe. The dredging head with suction pipe can be lowered to the required depth by a special support, which is situated in a well in the fore of the hull or on both sides of the ship. The holds are emptied either by pumping out or by opening their bottom. The operation of the dredging system and the ship itself is usually fully automatic and remote-controlled, which allows the supervising staff to watch the dredging process and the movement of the dredge from a specific point on the bridge.

Sea hoppers of this variety reach a length of 400 feet (120 metres) and need engines with an output of 8,000 h.p. They can dredge to a depth of 22 metres; the cubic capacity of their holds ranges from 4,000 to 6,000 cubic metres and their fully-laden speed averages 15 knots.

The Netherlands is the best known builder of all types of engineering craft and she exports suction dredgers all over the world.

THE SUBMARINE *NAUTILUS*

In addition to steam-driven, surface craft for civil and military purposes, Robert Fulton (1765–1815) also designed submarines. His first project was the construction of the submarine *Nautilus*, in Rouen in 1800. After trials on the Seine, the submarine was taken to Le Havre where successful diving and buoyancy tests were carried out. The *Nautilus* remained submerged with three men on board for more than two hours.

The length of the vessel was 21.25 feet (6.48 metres) and its maximum width was 6.36 feet (1.94 metres). The submarine was provided with horizontal and vertical rudders, and the anchor windlass was situated in the forward section of the hull. For movement on the surface, the *Nautilus* had a small mast with a detachable sail. Instead of an Archimedean screw it had a two-bladed, screw propeller, 4.39 feet (1.34 metres) in diameter. In addition, Fulton positioned another screw propeller with a vertical axis on the bow to improve stability when diving.

After tests, which involved the torpedoing of an old ship, had been successfully concluded, Fulton returned to Paris where, in 1801, he built a new *Nautilus* in the workshop of the Perrier Bros. The body of this submarine was spindle-shaped and had a shell made of copper plates. In July 1801 Fulton and his three companions carried out a series of successful trials with this new ship. The *Nautilus* dived to a depth of 25 feet (8 metres) and covered a distance of 440 yards in seven minutes. Equipped with reserves of compressed air, the crew remained submerged for 4 hours, 20 minutes. For torpedo action Fulton invented a torpedo filled with gunpowder and provided with a timing device. Using this, he sank an old shallop. Fulton failed to sell his invention to the French and disappointed, he returned to England in 1804 and later went to America.

Demologos was the first warship to be driven by steam. Her architect was again Robert Fulton. She was built in 1814 by Messrs. Adam and Noah Browne in New York and named *Fulton the First*. The ship was built to defend the coast and to break the British blockade of America. However, shortly after her initial outfit in September 1815 the war was over and thus the *Demologos*, to all intents and purposes never took part in the war. She was anchored in New York harbour and served as a store ship. An explosion in June 1829 completely destroyed her.

Demologos had a double wooden hull with a single deck. Between the two parallel keels there was a channel of some 15 feet, inside which the paddle wheel, which had a diameter of 16 feet and 10 radial paddles, was fitted. One part of the twin hull contained a 120 h.p. steam engine, the other contained a copper steam boiler. Twenty 32-pounders made up the ship's armament. Eight pieces were placed at each side, with two fore and two aft on the main deck, hidden behind a timber bulwark 58 inches (1.47 metres) thick. In July 1815 the *Demologos* made a successful maiden voyage, in which she reached a speed of 6.35 knots and covered 53 miles.

Dimensions: length 156 feet (47.5 metres), beam 56 feet (17.1 metres), depth 20 feet (6.10 metres), draught 10 feet (3.05 metres), deadweight 2,475 tons.

After the success of the steam-driven, double-deck, screw-propelled *Napoleon*, the ship designer, Dupuy de Lôme suggested the construction of a similar ship, but this time provided with armour. Thus in November 1859, the first armoured frigate, the *Gloire*, was born in the naval yards of Toulon. The basic construction was wooden, her displacement was 5,620 tons, she was fitted with a steam engine with a nominal output of 900 h.p. and during her trials she reached a speed of 13.5 knots. The screw propeller was four-bladed and had a diameter of 19 feet (5.8 metres). In addition to her steam engine, the *Gloire* was fore-and-aft rigged on all three masts, with three square sails on the fore and mainmasts and with two focs. The total surface area of the sails was 2,850 square metres. The armouring, consisting of forged iron plates, 4–5 inches (10–12 cm) thick, was fastened to both sides, two metres below the draught line. The fire power of the *Gloire* consisted of thirty-six 164-mm guns. Many other ships were built along the line of the *Gloire* in various countries in the second half of the nineteenth century.

Dimensions: length 255.7 feet (78 metres), beam 55.7 feet (17 metres), draught 25.4 feet (7.75 metres).

In August 1861, the Congress of the United States of America set up a commission to consider the suitability of building all-iron ships with gun batteries, called floating gun batteries. On the basis of the recommendation of the commission, three craft were built, the *New Ironsides* and the *Monitor*, which became the most famous. The *Monitor* was built to the design of the Swede, John Ericsson, who had successfully carried out trials with screw-propelled ships in England in the 1840s. The *Monitor* was raft-shaped with a revolving turret, twenty feet in diameter in which were mounted two 11-inch naval guns. The turret's plating was 8 inches (20 cm) thick. The hull was five inches thick. The ship was propelled by two screw propellers 9 feet (2.74 metres) in diameter. The steam engine was positioned in the hold of the ship below the water line.

The ship was built in the Greenpoint shipyard in New York and finished in the record time of 100 days. The *Monitor* was launched on 23 January 1862 and on 6 March, with a crew of 53, she left New York harbour to meet the *Merrimac* who had succeeded in a relatively short time in destroying several Federal craft. This first battle in history between two iron ships took place on 9 March 1862 in Hampton Roads in Virginia. Because of her better manoeuvrability, stronger armouring and low contours, the *Monitor* was able to defend herself against her three times more powerful rival without sustaining any serious damage. After a three hours' duel the *Merrimac* retreated. This battle of two armoured ships confirmed the advantage of revolving gun turrets, as well as the general construction of armoured, steam-driven and screw-propelled ships.

Dimensions: length 172 feet (52.5 metres), breadth 41.5 feet (12.65 metres), depth of hold 11.3 feet (3.45 metres), draught 10.5 feet (3.2 metres), displacement 1,200 tons.

The French made important advances in the building of submarines in the second half of the nineteenth century. In 1883 Dupuy de Lôme and Gustave Zédé began attempts to improve the submarine. For propulsion they intended to build a Captain Krebs electric motor which had been used in the first controlled zeppelin, La France. After Dupuy de Lôme's death, Gustave Zédé continued this work and in 1886, in the workshop of Forges and Chantiers de la Méditerranée, he built his first submarine. After demonstrating the submarine to the Admiralty he was asked to work out a new design, incorporating official suggestions. The result was the submarine *Gymnote*. Her keel was laid in the Toulon Arsenal in April 1887 and she was launched in September 1888. As yet she was not a real submarine weapon and the initial trials concentrated on the testing of the piping systems and the functioning of the electrical machinery.

The *Gymnote* had a symmetrical, spindle shape and later was equipped with a narrow deck for easier access. Her overall length was 56.4 feet (17.2 metres) and the hull at its largest point was 5.9 feet (1.8 metres) in diameter. She displaced some 29.3 tons, and her 55 h.p. electric motor was fed by 564 accumulators. Her shell was made up of rivetted, butt-joined steel plates.

After extensive trials over a period of two years, the Admiralty decided to order a larger submarine on the lines of the *Gymnote*. This was started in 1889 under the direction of G. Zédé and the engineer, Romazzotti. The new submarine was called the *Syrène* but after G. Zédé's death in 1891 she was renamed after him. The *Gymnote* and the *Gustave Zédé* remained the model for French submarines until the end of the nineteenth century.

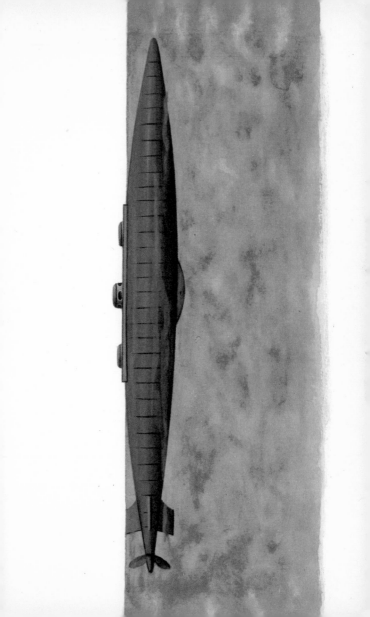

FIRST WORLD WAR SUBMARINE

By the end of the nineteenth century the main propulsion problem of the submarine was solved by using electric power for underwater navigation and the internal combustion engine for surface navigation. The greatest submarine navy in the First World War was owned by Germany. Its development began in 1902 with the construction of the experimental submarine *Forelle*, displacing some 16 tons and built according to the design of the engineer D'Equevilley. On the basis of successful trials with the *Forelle*, projects were started involving larger craft and the first submarines were ordered from abroad, by Russia. For propulsion, the design engineers used a petrol engine of the Körting type. In about 1910 diesel engines began to be used for sea-going vessels and soon this type of drive was also applied to the submarines.

Submarines of German design were built with a double shell. The interior shell was pressurised and

the exterior formed a cover for the water trimming tanks and the fuel tanks. The rudders for steering and vertical manoeuvres were placed in the stern. The submarine was generally propelled by screw propellers, driven by electric motors, which were fed by accumulators, when the ship was underwater, and by diesel engines when it was floating on the surface. In the turret placed amidships was the captain's lookout, provided with periscopes and snorkels ('sport' breathing tubes). The equipment of the submarine generally comprised four torpedo tubes in the bow and one or two in the stern, with possibly 7.5–16 cm guns and mine-laying equipment. German submarines of the First World War displaced 800 to 1,000 tons and were usually driven by two diesel engines generating in all 900–2,400 h.p. The diving depth was 30 to 75 metres, the surface speed was 18 knots, and when submerged 7.5 to 8.5 knots. The crew numbered 20 to 40.

In the 1880s when Whitehead improved the torpedo, it was found that the most suitable type of craft to carry this weapon was a small speed boat. The size of such boats steadily increased and by 1914 they were similar in shape to destroyers and closely resembled light cruisers. In wartime it was soon evident that guns were a more suitable armament for such craft than torpedoes.

At the beginning of the twentieth century the internal combustion engine had improved considerably and very soon came to be used in torpedo boats. Their relatively low speed remained an obstacle to further development. After numerous trials, Sir John I. Thornycroft solved the speed problem by designing the bottom of the boat in such a way that it slid over the water surface and in so doing improved its performance. In the summer of 1915 these designs were submitted to the British Admiralty

and as early as April 1916 the first coastal motor boats were produced with 250 h.p. engines. The boats were made of wood, were 40 feet long, armed with one torpedo, were manned by a crew of two and could travel at speeds of over 30 knots. They were used for the first time in 1916 during the bombardment of Ostende.

Subsequently such boats have been steadily improved. They have been extended to 55 feet and designed to carry two torpedoes, although later one of these was replaced by two depth charges. With a crew of five, these boats can now travel at 40 knots. At first they were mainly used against submarines and for coastal patrols but have been employed as minelayers and equipped with machine guns for defence against air attack. In the 1930s, they became the prototype for the development of fast torpedo boats.

THE BATTLESHIP DREADNOUGHT

The Russo-Japanese war and, in particular, the defeat of the Russian navy off Tsushima in 1905 had far-reaching consequences for the nature and role of battleships. Thereafter the main emphasis was put on firing capability and speed rather than on protective armour.

Great Britain was the first country to capitalise on this experience by building the battleship *Dreadnought*. The ship was started in October 1905 in the state-owned Portsmouth Dockyard and was finished in the record time of one year. In February 1906 the *Dreadnought* was launched and commissioned within the year. The ship carried ten 12-inch guns (305 mm) in five twin-turrets, of which four could always provide flanking fire. The gun turrets were situated higher than usual and so facilitated more accurate long-distance fire. In the waterline section of her hull, the *Dreadnought* was armoured by plates 28 cm thick, but in the bow by only 15-cm plates and in the stern by 10-cm ones. This armouring became insufficient in the course of time. In addition to her 12-inch guns, the *Dreadnought* also had twenty-four 3-inch guns (76 mm) and five torpedo tubes below water. She was protected against enemy torpedoes by the usual nets, suspended from rotating arms. Four sets of Parsons steam turbines with a total output of 24,700 h.p. were used as a new type of mechanical propulsion. The speed of the ship was on average 21.5 knots.

Dimensions: length o.a. 526 feet (160.1 metres), beam 82 feet (25 metres), maximum draught 31 feet (9.5 metres), displacement 22,500 tons. The crew numbered 800.

The battleship *West Virginia* and her sister ships, the *Maryland* and the *Colorado*, were built close after the First World War in the North American shipyard of Newport News. The ship was laid down in April 1920 and was finished in December 1923. In design she was similar to the 'California' class of battleship. The characteristic feature of these ships was their slender funnels and two tower masts of grid construction. The *West Virginia* was built with lessons learned during the First World War very much in mind, and therefore she had more powerful armouring along the water line and a more efficient gun battery of eight 16-inch guns (40.6 cm) with a range of 33,300 yards (30 km), placed in four twin-turrets, fore and aft. In addition the ship had twelve 5-inch guns (12.7 cm), 8 anti-aircraft guns of the same size, eleven 1.5-inch (4 cm) anti-aircraft machine guns and two underwater tubes for 21-inch torpedoes (533 mm). She carried three hydroplanes and two aircraft catapults. The gun turrets and the guns were electrically controlled, as were the elevators. The battleship *West Virginia* had four screw propellers driven by General Electric steam turbines, developing a total of 27,300 h.p. Steam was supplied by eight Babcock-Wilcox boilers. In trials she attained a speed of 21 knots.

Dimensions: length o.a. 624 feet (190.2 metres), beam 97.5 feet (29.7 metres), maximum draught 35 feet (10.7 metres), crew 1,486 men.

The *Yamato* and her sister ship, *Musashi*, were the greatest battleships ever built in the world. The project was initiated in 1934 when military circles in Japan started to prepare seriously for a conflict with the U.S.A. The construction of the ships began in 1937 in the yards of the Mitsubishi firm in Nagasaki. They were launched in 1940 and commissioned in 1941. The ships had a divided and flared bow, a powerful fore superstructure with tower mast, one funnel amidships and a main deck that narrowed gradually. Their armament consisted of nine 18-inch (457 mm) guns situated in three turrets (two fore and one aft), twelve 6.1-inch (155 mm) guns and twelve 25-mm anti-aircraft guns. In addition to these guns, the ships had eight 609-mm torpedo tubes. Two catapults designed for seven aircraft were placed amidships. The armouring of the ships was similarly unusual and particularly strong. Instead of several armoured decks of various thicknesses, both battleships had a single deck, the armour plates of which were 212 mm thick, and the sides were protected by plates 410 mm thick and the gun turrets with 650-mm armour plates. Four Japanese-made steam turbines, generating in all 150,000 h.p., propelled the ship, giving her a maximum speed of 27 knots. The battleship *Yamato* was sunk in April 1945 on her way to Okinawa to relieve army units. She was hit seven times by heavy bombs and torpedoed on twelve occasions.

Dimensions: length o.a. 862.3 feet (263 metres), beam 121 feet (36.9 metres), draught 35.7 feet (10.9 metres), displacement fully-laden 72,809 tons, crew 2,500 men.

At the beginning of the twentieth century a new type of a ship was developed, based on experience derived from the battle off Tsushima. This was the battle cruiser, a ship with the armaments of a standard battleship but with a higher speed, facilitating the encirclement of the enemy. British ships of the 1908 'Invincible' class, the 1912 'Indefatigable' class and the German cruisers *Von der Tann*, *Goeben*, *Lützow* and others were some of these first battle cruisers.

The greatest battle cruiser and, until the Second World War, the greatest warship in the world was the *Hood*. Her construction was begun in 1916 in the John Brown shipyards at Clydebank. In August 1918 she was launched and finally completed in March 1920. Her armament consisted of eight 15-inch guns (380 mm) placed in four turrets; two fore and two aft with a possible 150° rotation on each side; there were also further twelve 5.5-inch guns (140 mm), four anti-aircraft 4-inch guns (102 mm) and other smaller weapons. The torpedo equipment of the *Hood* consisted of two underwater and four surface 21-inch

torpedo tubes (533 mm). The deck was equipped with a catapult and one hydroplane. The sides of the vessel had 12.7-inch and 5-inch thick (26.25 cm and 12.7 cm) steel plates, while under the water line they were three inches thick (7.62 cm). The turrets were armoured with 15- and 12-inch plates (38 and 30.5 cm) and the deck had 2- and 3-inch (5 and 6.6 cm) plating.

The four screw propellers were driven by Brown-Curtis steam turbines, developing a total of 144,000 h.p. Steam was supplied by 24 short-tube Yarrow boilers, heated by oil. The maximum speed of the ship was 31 knots. The *Hood* was sunk on 24 May 1941, southwest of Iceland, in a battle with the German battleship *Bismarck*, after her ammunition stock received a direct hit.

Dimensions: length o.a. 860 feet (262 metres), beam 105 feet 2½ inches (32.1 metres), draught 31.5 feet (9.6 metres), displacement 42,100 tons, crew 1,341 men.

Aircraft carriers were used a little even in the First World War. The great naval powers soon realised their future importance and therefore the Washington Treaty of 1922 included these ships in the rules prescribing the permitted naval ratios, although before this date they had been owned only by Great Britain. Japan was the first to build aircraft carriers but the U.S.A. soon joined in and Great Britain also built more powerful ones, so that by the beginning of the Second World War, Great Britain had seven aircraft carriers, and the U.S.A. and Japan each had six. The importance of aircraft carriers was confirmed in the course of the Second World War when aircraft, taking off from their decks, decided the battle off Midway, which concluded the war in the Pacific. After the war, naval designers concentrated on increasing engine power and on adapting carriers for a greater number of faster and heavier aircraft. The culmination of these efforts was the construction of the U.S. carrier *Enterprise*, which is driven by nuclear power. The keel was laid in February 1958 in the Newport News yards and the *Enterprise* was finished in December 1961. In 1965 the ship joined the U.S. Pacific fleet.

Her aircraft deck has a surface of 4.5 acres and carries 70 to 100 aircraft, which are brought up to the deck by four elevators. The *Enterprise* has no funnels and the tower superstructure carries radar scanners, aerials, remote control devices and the deck gear control. Four screw propellers are driven by steam turbines, developing 300,000 h.p. The steam is supplied by eight nuclear reactors cooled by pressurised water. The average speed of the ship is 33 knots and the operational radius at this speed is 140,000 sea miles.

Dimensions: length o.a. 1,123 feet (341 metres), beam 133 feet (40.5 metres), draught 37 feet (11.3 metres), width of the flight deck 257 feet (78.3 metres), displacement 75,700 tons, crew 2,870 men, flying crew 1,430 men.

HEADY CRUISER

HEAVY CRUISER

The Washington Treaty, signed after the First World War, determined the tonnage and numbers of great warships and limited the displacement of cruisers to 10,000 tons and stated that their guns should not exceed 8 inches (200 mm). The London Conference of 1930 divided cruisers into heavy (with guns exceeding 6.1 inch (155 mm)) and light categories and limited their respective tonnage and the number of such craft owned by the three naval powers, the U.S.A., Great Britain and Japan. This division of cruisers quickly became commonplace in the navies of the world. Before the Second World War, this group of heavy cruisers comprised the British ships *Exeter*, *York*, *Suffolk*, *Kent*, and *Dorsetshire*; the French 'Algerie' class, the American 'Indianapolis' class, the German ships the *Admiral Hipper* and *Prinz Eugen*; the Italian 'Zara' class and others.

Before and during the war some of the cruisers were remodelled as anti-aircraft vessels. The Swedish cruiser, *Göta Leyon*, of the 'Tre Kronor' class, was designed as an anti-aircraft ship. Her keel was laid in September 1943 in the Eriksberg Mekaniska Verkstad shipyard in Gothenburg. She was completed in December 1947 and rebuilt between 1951 and 1952. Her armament consists of seven 6-inch anti-aircraft guns (152 mm), four 2.2-inch guns (57 mm) and eleven 40-mm machine guns. In addition this cruiser has six 21-inch (533 mm) torpedo tubes and is equipped to lay mines. Her two screw propellers are driven by two De Laval steam turbines, generating in whole 100,000 h.p.

Dimensions: length o.a. 597 feet (182 metres), beam 54 feet (16.5 metres), draught 21.3 feet (6.5 metres), displacement 9,200 tons, crew 610 men.

MISSILE CRUISER

In the fifties of this century newly-developed missile weapons were introduced into the navy. The existing cruisers, destroyers and frigates were rebuilt and new ones designed to take guided missiles. A purpose-built missile cruiser is the U.S. nuclear-powered ship *Long Beach*. The project was developed by the U.S. Navy Bureau of Ships. The keel of the cruiser was laid in December 1957 in the naval yards of Bethlehem Steel Co. in Quincy and the ship was finished in September 1961. In 1966 she was put into active service in the Pacific. She is the first nuclear-powered surface warship.

The *Long Beach* has two Westinghouse nuclear reactors, which are cooled by pressurised water and which supply the steam for the turbines, which can reach 80,000 h.p. The ship has two screw propellers and in her trials she attained a speed of 30.5 knots. Under full power she can sail 100,000 miles.

Her armament consists of one twin Talos missile launcher, placed aft, two Terrier launchers placed fore and one Asroc launcher amidships. On top of this the *Long Beach* has two single 5-inch guns (127 mm) against surface targets and six 12-inch torpedo tubes (305 mm) on the main deck.

Dimensions: length o.a. 721.2 feet (219.8 metres), beam 73.2 feet (22.3 metres), draught 32.2 feet (9.8 metres), displacement 14,200 tons, crew 985 men.

This type of light cruiser started at the beginning of the twentieth century as a ship which worked with torpedo boats and gave them protection in case of attack by enemy ships. Light cruisers were armoured not only on their decks but also at their sides. Their steam turbines gave them the necessary higher speed. The size of their guns gradually increased up to 6-inch (152 mm). At the outbreak of the First World War their average displacement was 3,500 tons and their speed about 28 knots. They were named after towns. Similar ships built at the end of the First World War had reached a displacement of 5,000 tons and became then the standard type of light cruiser.

The *Ajax* of the 'Leander' class was a type of light cruiser of the pre-Second World War period. She was built in the Vickers Armstrong yard in Barrow and finished in June 1935. Her armament consisted of eight 6-inch (152 mm) guns placed in four turrets, four 4-inch (92 mm) anti-aircraft guns and other

smaller guns. In addition *Ajax* was equipped with eight torpedo tubes and carried two aircraft on board. The armouring of the sides was 2–4 inches (5–10 cm) thick, the turrets and the bridge had 1-inch (2.5 cm) plating and the deck was made of steel plates, 2 inches thick (5 cm).

The *Ajax* was driven by Parsons steam turbines, which generated 72,000 h.p. and drove four screw propellers. Steam was supplied by four admiralty-type boilers. The speed of the ship was 32.5 knots. In the Second World War the *Ajax* took part in the battle against the German battleship, the *Admiral Graf Spee*, in December 1939 off Montevideo. She was also in action against the Italian navy in the Mediterranean in 1940 and in 1941 took part in the evacuation of British troops from Greece and Crete.

Dimensions: length 522 feet (159.2 metres), beam 55.6 feet (17 metres), draught 15.5 feet (4.7 metres), displacement 6,840 tons, crew 550 men.

THE NUCLEAR-POWERED SUBMARINE *NAUTILUS*

The first ship to use nuclear power was the *Nautilus*, named after Verne's and Fulton's submarines. She was started in 1952 in the naval yards of the Electric Boat Co. in Groton, Connecticut and in 1955 she was delivered to the U. S. Navy. In the first years of her operation the piping and propulsion systems were tested.

The hull of the *Nautilus* is cigar-shaped and she has a pronounced bow. The thermal power is supplied by the nuclear reactor, which is cooled by pressu sed water. The fuel is enriched uranium, U 235. In the boiler the cooling water transfers heat to the second water circuit where steam is produced, building up to seventeen times normal atmospheric pressure and a temperature of 213°C. The steam is used to run the steam turbines which are provided with reduction gear and drive two screw propellers. In addition to nuclear drive, the *Nautilus* is equipped

with a normal diesel engine. The total output of the engines is approximately 15,000 h.p. The reserves of nuclear power guarantee independent navigation for 70,000 sea miles (130,000 km). Underwater the *Nautilus* can reach a speed of 20 knots, and on the surface 25 knots is possible. The *Nautilus* may spend fifty days underwater without interruption. The maximum diving depth is 750 feet (230 metres). Her armaments consist of six torpedo tubes located at the bow. In 1958 the *Nautilus*, with a crew of 116 men, sailed from Puget Sound in the Pacific Ocean under the North Pole to England. During this voyage, which took 22 days, the *Nautilus* remained nearly 90 hours under water. She passed under the North Pole on 3 August.

Dimensions: length 321 feet (98 metres), beam 28 feet (8.5 metres), displacement 3,180 tons, crew 101 men.

In the 1860s the torpedo was invented in Austria and in a short time was introduced into most European navies. Subsequently torpedo boats were equipped with torpedoes and reached a speed of 18 knots. Their number and size increased and to counteract them it was necessary to build stronger and faster warships. The torpedo-boat destroyer, which was developed in 1893 by Yarrow, displacing 220 tons and capable of 27 knots, was such a craft. The introduction of steam turbines, the invention of C. Parsons, increased this speed to 30 knots. At the beginning of the twentieth century the torpedo boat and the torpedo-boat destroyer merged together into one type of warship displacing about 450 tons.

After the Russo-Japanese war the torpedo-boat destroyers grew from 900 to 1,100 tons. The introduction of oil-fired steam boilers made it possible to use more efficient turbines and thus reach even higher speeds. In addition to four to twelve torpedo tubes, the torpedo-boat destroyers usually carried three to five guns. After the First World War when

this type of large torpedo-boat destroyer settled down at about 1,300 tons, their gun calibre gradually increased to 120 and 138 mm, as did the calibre of the torpedo tubes, whilst their speed rose from 35 to 40 knots. In the course of the Second World War torpedo-boat destroyers were used as escort craft for the protection of convoys against air attack, submarines and other torpedo craft.

After the Second World War the design of the torpedo-boat destroyers was substantially changed. Normal torpedoes were replaced by anti-submarine torpedoes. The number of guns was reduced and sometimes they were replaced by missile launchers. Their displacement reached 2,500 tons and their speed remained at between 35 to 40 knots.

An example of such an anti-submarine destroyer is the Dutch *Overijssel* of the 'Friesland' class, which displaces 2,497 tons and is equipped with two depth charge mortars, eight anti-submarine torpedo tubes and anti-submarine rocket throwers.

In the seventeenth century the term 'frigate' was used for the three-masted sailing ship with one covered gun deck. Later they were employed as patrol and communication vessels. During the nineteenth century they passed through the same development as other warships; they were armoured, steam-driven, had screw propulsion and gave rise to the armoured cruiser. The name 'frigate' began to be used again during the Second World War for smaller warships with anti-submarine armament and light guns, which were used to escort convoys instead of the fast escort boats and corvettes which had hitherto been used. While corvettes were relatively small ships similar to whalers, were capable of 15 knots and armed with one naval gun, several anti-aircraft guns and depth charges, frigates displaced about 1,350 tons and could reach a speed of approximately 20 knots. In addition to more powerful guns

they had bomb throwers and a considerable supply of normal depth charges.

After the Second World War frigates were subdivided according to their specialised purpose. There are: general purpose frigates, fast frigates, anti-aircraft and anti-submarine frigates equipped with missile launchers; and there are frigates with a specialist task, such as aircraft control. Some of these types weigh up to 2,000 tons and have a speed of 40 knots, so that they are indistinguishable from torpedo-boat destroyers.

An example of a fast frigate is the French *La Corse*, which weighs 1,290 tons and was built in the Lorient naval yards between 1951 and 1955. In addition to the normal gun batteries she has one sextuple missile launcher, charge mortars and twelve torpedo tubes. Her Rateau A & C turbines generate some 20,000 h.p. and give her a maximum speed of 28.5 knots. Crew numbers 174 men.

MINESWEEPER

Minesweepers, like minelayers, belong to a specialised group of warships. Various craft, great and small, can be used for the destruction and laying of mines, if they have the proper equipment. During the First and Second World Wars specially-built ships or miscellaneous craft, such as fishing trawlers and cutters were used to destroy mines. The destruction procedure varies according to the type of mine. These are either contact, magnetic or acoustic mines. Most mines are anchored in a predetermined position and float at a certain depth under the surface. They are released from their anchorage in a number of ways: for example, minesweepers sail side by side, towing an arched, sweep wire, which cuts through the anchoring ropes of the mines, or else paravanes, which were invented in 1917, are used. These are remote-control floating shark- or torpedo-shaped devices, which float at a certain depth and distance from both sides of the ship. By means of sweeping wires, which

connect them one to another, they free the anchored mines. The mines are destroyed when they surface. Paravanes are used by war and merchant ships to ensure essential protection against mines. A third system of mine destruction relies on a special sweeping float called Oropesa sweep. The float is towed behind the minesweeper and to the sweep wire are attached special kites (otters) which keep the wire taut and at the predetermined depth beneath the surface.

Minesweepers are small craft of some 400 to 800 tons and are sometimes made of wood or other anti-magnetic material. The towing winch is placed behind the superstructure, similar to the towing hook of tugs. The stern is equipped with a crane or a boom to raise and lower floats. The mines are destroyed by small calibre, naval guns. For protection against air raids minesweepers are equipped with smaller guns and machine guns.

244

FAST TORPEDO AND PATROL BOAT

This type of fast boat was developed before the Second World War from the English coastal torpedo boat. Such speed boats displaced about 100 tons, were fitted out with torpedo tubes on both sides and a heavy 20-mm machine gun, were manned by a crew of 17 and could travel at 35 knots. They were entirely steel-constructed. In the course of the war further design improvements enabled the boats to operate on the open sea. Their displacement increased to 120 tons and their armaments were extended by one 40-mm gun and two to three 20-mm guns, and their speed rose from 35 to 40 knots. They were driven by diesel engines, generating 3,000 h.p. After the war their design improved, particularly their power and speed. They are now equipped with gas turbines with an output of 5,000

h.p. Their superstructure is usually made of aluminium alloys and their armaments strengthened by anti-aircraft and machine guns.

Similar to these boats are the various patrol boats used by the navy and customs services. The armament of such patrol boats varies according to their purpose and area of operation, but is mostly limited to small-calibre guns and multi-rifled machine guns.

An example of this kind of boat is the fast patrol boat of the Royal Navy's 'Brave' class, displacing 89 tons and driven by a gas turbine. She can be used as a motor torpedo boat, armed with four 21-inch torpedoes (533 mm) and one 40-mm single Bofors gun or as a gun-boat with two Bofors guns and two 40-mm single torpedoes. Such a boat is capable of 50 knots.

LIST OF TABLES

LIST OF ILLUSTRATED SHIPS